PORTRAIT OF THE CHANNEL ISLANDS

By the same author

History of the Channel Islands

ILLUSTRATIONS

MAPS

I

FACE OF THE ISLANDS—I

O! ever happy isles, your heads so high that rear,
By nature strongly fenced, which never need to fear;
On Neptune's wat'ry realms, when Æolus raised wars,
And every billow bounds as though to quench the stars.
Fair Jersey, first of these, here scattered in the deep
Peculiarly that boasts thy double horned sheep. , . .
                              Michael Drayton (1563–1631)

The Bailiwick of Jersey comprises the Island of Jersey, two groups of islets—the Ecréhous and the Minquiers, commonly pronounced 'Ek-cree-hose' and 'Minkies'—as well as other smaller islets and rocks in the vicinity. British sovereignty over the Ecréhous and Minquiers was confirmed in 1953 by judgment of the International Court of Justice at The Hague. The coast of France lies close by, and the shortest distance between that country and Jersey is only 15 miles, the coast of the Continent being clearly visible from the eastern side of the island. "*Morceaux de France tombés à la mer et ramassés par l'Angleterre*" ("Pieces of France fallen into the sea and gathered up by England") was the delightful way in which Victor Hugo described how the Channel Islands, though so near to France, are, nevertheless, British. Jersey is inhabited, but, although there are buildings on the Ecréhous and Minquiers, they are used only for short periods by such people as fishermen. Jersey's area is 45 square miles and, although heavily built over, the island still contains quite a large amount of agricultural land. It slopes from north to south into the sun, and the Gulf Stream flows in its direction to make the climate milder than it otherwise would be; snow rarely settles for any length of time; the prevailing wind is south-west, but at certain times of the year the wind blows steadily from the east. Jersey is divided into twelve parishes, namely: Grouville, St.

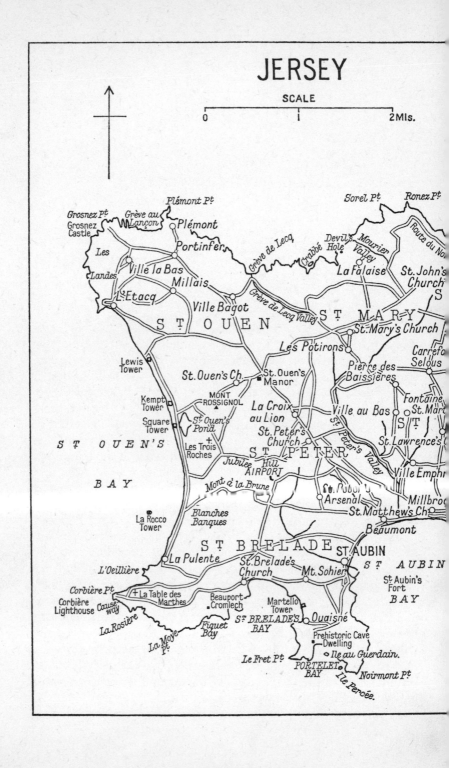

JERSEY

SCALE

0   1   2 MIs.

Plémont Pt.

Sorel Pt.   Ronez Pt.

Grosnez Pt.
Grosnez
Castle

Grève au
Lançon

Plémont

Devil's
Hole

Mourier
Valley

Route du Nord

Les
Landes

Portinfer

Grève de Lecq

Crabbé

La Falaise

St. John's
Church

Ville la Bas

Grève de Lecq Valley

S

Millais

St. Mary's Church

L'Etacq

Ville Bagot

S T . O U E N

S T . M A R Y

Les Potirons

Carrefo
Selous

Lewis
Tower

St. Ouen's Ch.

St. Ouen's
Manor

Pierre des
Baissières

Ville au Bas

Fontaine
St. Mart

Kempt
Tower

MONT
ROSSIGNOL

La Croix
au Lion

St. Peter's Valley

S T

Square
Tower

St. Ouen's
Pond

St. Peter's
Church

St. Lawrence's

ST. OUEN'S

Les Trois
Roches

Jubilee
Hill

S T . P E T E R

Ville Emph

Mont à la Brune

AIRPORT

BAY

St. Robert

Arsenal

Millbro

La Rocco
Tower

Blanches
Banques

St. Matthew's Ch

Beaumont

S T. B R E L A D E

St. Aubin

ST. AUBIN

L'Oeillière

La Pulente

St. Brelade's
Church

Mt. Sohier

St. Aubin's
Fort

BAY

Corbière Pt.

Corbière
Lighthouse

Cause-
way

La Table des
Marthes

Beauport
Cromlech

Martello
Tower

Ouaisné

La Rosière

Figuet
Bay

ST. BRELADE'S
BAY

Prehistoric Cave
Dwelling

La Moye
Pt.

Le Fret Pt.

Ile au Guerdain.

PORTELET
BAY

Noirmont Pt.

Ile Percée.

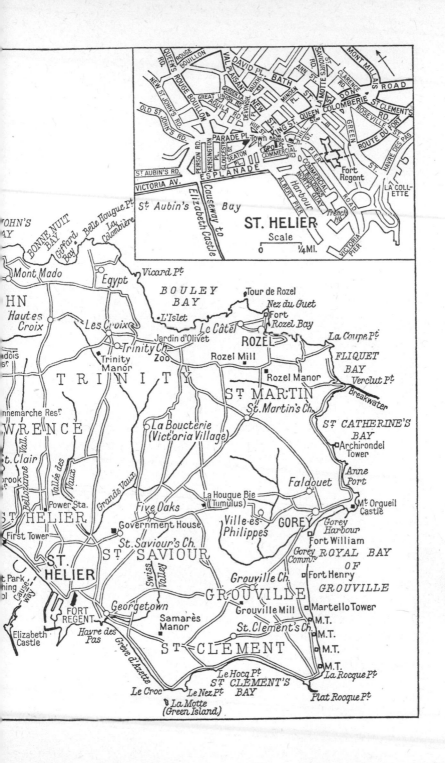

ST. HELIER

Scale

0   ¼ MI.

Brelade, St. Clement, St. Helier, St. John, St. Lawrence, St. Martin, St. Mary, St. Ouen, St. Peter, St. Saviour and Trinity. Each parish partly borders the sea—in the case of St. Saviour for only a very short distance, but St. Peter has two seaboards, on the south and on the west.

There are many excellent sandy beaches, the most popular of which are the Royal Bay of Grouville, St. Aubin's Bay (compared favourably with the Bay of Naples), St. Brelade's Bay (somewhat dangerous for bathing towards its eastern end), St. Clement's Bay and St. Ouen's Bay (excellent for surf bathing, but somewhat dangerous in parts). The West Park area of St. Aubin's Bay is particularly popular, as are St. Brelade's Bay, Havre des Pas and Portelet Bay, all in the south, and, in the north, Grève de Lecq, with its beautiful reddish coloured sand. Numerous other bays are frequented to a greater or lesser extent, but the local people have their favourites, which are generally the more secluded.

Fine cliffs on the south-west and north coasts are riddled with caves estimated to number more than 300; the best known are La Cotte de St. Brelade (or La Cotte à la Fée), Ouaisné, St. Brelade, La Cotte à la Chèvre and those at Grève au Lançon, to the east of Grosnez, St. Ouen, and La Belle Hougue, Trinity. In front of one of the caves at Grève au Lançon stands the Needle Rock, some 60 to 70 feet high. At least two of the island's caves contain stalactites.

There are a few islets close inshore, those in St. Aubin's Bay being the best known—L'Islet, on which stands Elizabeth Castle; the Hermitage Rock (connected to the former by a breakwater) and the islet on which St. Aubin's Fort is built. In Portelet Bay is the Ile au Guerdain, sometimes referred to as Janvrin's Tomb because Captain Philip Janvrin was buried there temporarily in 1721, after dying of the plague aboard his ship; the tower was built on the islet in 1808. In the middle of St. Ouen's Bay there is an islet on which stands La Rocco Tower (1795–1801), originally called Fort Gordon. The Germans used the tower as a target for gunnery practice during the Occupation, and it was considerably damaged; further damage by the sea was caused in the ensuing years, and at one time it seemed that it would be totally destroyed. Fortunately, however, La Rocco Tower was saved at the eleventh hour by the States with the help of funds raised by a public appeal. On the north coast is the Ile Agois, an isolated mass of rock at Crabbé, separated from the mainland by a narrow gorge. In Bonne Nuit Bay is the rock known as Le Cheval Guillaume, and in Bouley Bay is L'Islet. Off the east coast is L'Avarison, an islet where stands Seymour Tower (1782), which, unlike other similar fortifications, is square in shape. Some say that the original tower, erected about 1540, was named after Sir Edward Seymour, a governor of the island; others that the present tower was named after Marshal Conway, a later governor, one of whose forenames was Seymour. In St. Clement's Bay are La Motte (commonly called Green Island), a prehistoric site, and Icho Island, on which stands Icho Tower.

Leaving the town of St. Helier (see Chapter VI) and proceeding along the Esplanade westwards there are two alternative routes: the first by Victoria Avenue and the second by St. Aubin's Road, the two roads converging at Bel Royal, St. Lawrence. A fine marine promenade stretches from the harbour entrance along the Albert Pier as far as the little town of St. Aubin. At the West Park end of the avenue is a granite pedestal surmounted by a crown and inscribed "Victoria Avenue 22nd June, 1897". From the avenue looking to the east are the Town Hill and the harbour, to the south Elizabeth Castle and St. Aubin's Fort and to the west a distant view of Noirmont headland. St. Aubin's Road starts by skirting to the right the foot of the pine-covered slopes of Westmount and to the left the Lower Park; the road continues past the King George V Memorial Homes and the Animals' Cemetery (1928) and then moves through the suburb known as First Tower, which took its name from the martello tower situated in the vicinity.

On the right are the Sun Works (where tea is blended, packed and exported to most parts of the world) and First Tower Park, in which is St. Andrew's Church. The road then passes through Millbrook, with Villa Millbrook on the right and St. Matthew's, the so-called 'Glass Church' (see Chapter VIII) and Coronation Park (1937) on the left. Villa Millbrook was the residence of the first Baron Trent of Nottingham, founder of 'Boots' the chemists, who is buried on the cliffs beyond St. Brelade's Church. St. Aubin's Road then proceeds to Bel Royal where 'Maison Charles' and the house known as 'Bel Royal' form the corner with St. Peter's Valley Road. On the gable of 'Bel Royal', facing St.

Aubin's Road, there is a sundial dated 1794; a second martello tower once stood nearby but was destroyed in 1943 during the German Occupation.

When the road reaches Beaumont, another, called Beaumont Hill, branches inland and leads to the airport. A short way up the hill, in the apex of its junction with Old Beaumont Hill, is to be found, suitably mounted under a thatched canopy, a bronze falconet, 7 feet 3 inches long with a calibre of 2·8 inches and weighing 7½ hundredweight; it was made for the parish of St. Peter by John Owen in 1551.

The coast road then proceeds through Beaumont—where there is another martello tower—to St. Aubin, passing on the right the 'Forester's Arms', a public-house reputed to have been established in 1717, and then the property called 'Merman', occupying the site of Merman Cottage, where Lillie Langtry once lived. The cottage was named after her horse, which won the Cesarewitch in 1897 and gained for her the sum of £39,000. The road then continues westward and passes La Haule Manor, now a hotel, until it reaches St. Aubin (see Chapter VI). To the south of the town is Noirmont headland, Belcroute Bay, Portelet Bay and Ouaisné Bay. Just by Belcroute Bay is Noirmont Manor.

The headland is a splendid unspoilt stretch of heath with commanding views; this belongs to the States, its purchase having been approved on 26th September 1946, as the island's memorial of World War II. German fortifications, grim reminders of the Occupation, scar the headland, and at its southern tip, just above the sea, is a tower, La Tour de Vinde (1810–14). From St. Aubin a pleasant footpath follows the line of the old railway track to Corbière.

The main road as it turns inland from St. Aubin climbs Mont les Vaux, passing on the left in a recess nearly opposite St. Aubin's Church an old public pump dated 1862, and then swings south to reach Seven Oaks. It passes over the tunnel of the old railway and turns west just before Mont Sohier; here there is a fork, and one road goes to the right to reach the district known as Red Houses, while the other runs southwards down into St. Brelade's Bay. Here are two more martello towers; Le Château des Roches, where General Boulanger (1837–91) stayed when he sought refuge in Jersey in 1889; and St. Brelade's Church and the Fishermen's Chapel in their incomparable setting.

A promenade constructed along the top of the sea wall built by the Germans during the Occupation skirts part of the bay, and on the sea front is a small and beautifully kept ornamental garden with a fountain. On the inland side of the road is the Churchill Memorial Park, opened in 1966, containing a memorial to Sir Winston Churchill, which takes the form of a rough-hewn block of grey granite with plaque and inscription. To the south-west of the church are three bays—Bouilly Port, Beau Port and Fiquet Bay. The land adjacent to Beau Port was presented to the States by the second Lord Trent in 1948 and is known as the Joyce Trent Park. The road through St. Brelade's Bay turns inland just past the church and proceeds by way of La Marquanderie Hill to Red Houses.

Some distance up the hill on the left is a wayside fountain and drinking trough dated 1834, with the carving of a cow's head. Since 1945 there has been a tremendous amount of development in this district and almost a new town has grown up. La Route Orange runs from Red Houses westwards and links with the road leading to La Pulente and St. Ouen's Bay. Another road leads to Corbière with its famous and much photographed lighthouse (see Chapter VIII). Two bays lie between Fiquet Bay and Corbière— La Rosière and Petit Port. In the old quarry at La Rosière is the desalination plant of The Jersey New Waterworks Co. Ltd.

From Corbière a road runs east and connects with the road for La Pulente. The approach to La Pulente from the east presents a splendid view of St. Ouen's Bay—in fact it can be described as breathtaking, especially on a rough day when the breakers come crashing in. A similar splendid view may be obtained from the Mont du Vallet approach at the northern end of the bay. From La Pulente, all along the bay, runs the Five Mile Road (La Route des Mielles), which, incidentally, is not five miles long; the beach is excellent and the wild scenery most attractive. Both ends of the bay are good places for collecting seaweed (known locally as *vraic*), and there are a number of slipways for lorries to obtain access to the beach, notably those at Mont du Feu, Les Brayes, L'Ouzière, La Crabière and Les Laveurs.

All along the bay are scattered defences dating from the eighteenth century to the German Occupation. The former comprise, from south to north, a martello tower, La Tour Carrée (1778), Kempt Tower (1834) and Lewis Tower (1835), named after Lieutenant-Colonel G. G. Lewis, its designer. Towards the centre of the bay on the landward side of the road is La Mare au Seigneur (commonly called St. Ouen's Pond), which, by courtesy of the Seigneur of St. Ouen, is in the care of the Société Jersiaise, who use it as a nature reserve and bird-ringing station. The island in the centre is reputed to be prehistoric in origin, and the reed-fringed pond, the largest natural expanse of fresh water in the Channel Islands, contains carp.

Towards the northern end of the bay the road swings inland and then turns back towards L'Etacq, from which point roads run north to Grosnez, Portinfer and Plémont. There is a peat-bed on the beach at L'Etacq, made use of during the German Occupation. To the west lies Les Landes, a large (for Jersey) expanse of heathland, covered in gorse and heather, where, overhanging the sea, is the Pinnacle Rock, on the landward side of which is a prehistoric site. To the north lie the remains of Grosnez Castle (see Chapter VIII) and the lighthouse on Grosnez Point, excellent places from which to view the sunset.

The high cliffs stretching nearly the whole length of the north of the island provide splendid views not only along the coast but also out to sea and, depending on the weather, views can be obtained of Guernsey and Sark to the west, Alderney to the north and the French coast to the east. Vegetation clothing the upper parts of the cliffs changes colour according to season—the bracken sprouts pale green in spring, turning as the year advances to a darker shade of green with a gloss finish, while in the autumn dark green gives way to brown; splashes of bright gold are provided by prickly gorse and drifts of purple by the heather. Cliff paths make this beauty accessible to those prepared to abandon cars and walk.

To the east of Grosnez are Grève au Lançon and Plémont. Portinfer is the hub of the district, and no fewer than six roads converge at this spot. From there the main road (known at this point as Vinchelez Lane) runs past Vinchelez de Bas Manor and Vinchelez de Haut Manor. A left fork leads down into Grève de Lecq with yet another martello tower; the attractive old Moulin de Lecq still retains its mill-wheel but is now converted into an inn. At one time a camera obscura was located in the bay. Grève de Lecq Valley is wooded and generally unspoilt; to the north lies Crabbé, with its rifle range, and the fine headland of Col de la

Rocque, a property belonging to The National Trust for Jersey.

Side roads lead to Le Creux de Vis (commonly called the Devil's Hole), a great opening behind the cliff eroded by the sea, where an effigy of the devil has been kept since 1851, the first of the series being converted from a ship's figurehead. The sea enters by means of a natural blow-hole or channel. Other by-roads lead further east to Sorel and Ronez, with its vast quarry works, and from there La Route du Nord winds along the cliff top, on the sea side just before Frémont being the Wolf Caves. Near Frémont is the Independent Television Authority's mast.

The road now descends into Bonne Nuit Bay with its picturesque harbour and La Crête Fort (1835) at its eastern end. The road then climbs up to Les Platons, the highest part of Jersey, reaching 446 feet. In this area can be seen, fairly close together, the masts of Rediffusion (Jersey) Ltd., B.B.C. Television and the Decca Navigator Radio Transmitting Station. At the foot of the cliffs lie Giffard Bay and Petit Port. The road proceeds past Egypt, Tas de Geon and Les Hurels, the view over the wooded locality of Egypt being truly delightful. Bouley Bay and its harbour are then reached where the steep and winding road serves as the course for a National Hill Climb held annually under the auspices of the Jersey Motor Cycle and Light Car Club.

Leaving this beautiful bay, in an easterly direction, the coast road generally follows the line of the cliffs but is a little inland. To the north lie La Tête des Hougues, L'Etacquerel and Le Câtel. Rozel Valley runs into Rozel, a delightful little place with a harbour, an old barracks (now a hotel) and a number of old granite-built houses and cottages. The grounds of the property Château La Chaire were laid out last century and planted with unusual trees and shrubs; a fine magnolia tree is visible from the lane which passes in front of the property and presents a beautiful sight when in bloom. The main road continues through Rozel, still going east and then swings south. To the north-east lies Douet de la Mer, then come Le Couperon, Le Saie Harbour and La Coupe Point, a left turn leading to Fliquet Bay. Close by is Rozel Manor House, standing in its spacious grounds.

From Fliquet Bay, with its old martello tower and stony beach, it is possible to work around to St. Catherine's Breakwater, where a good view may be obtained of the Ecréhous; this truly magnificent breakwater (1847–55) serves as a promenade and is a popular place for angling. From St. Catherine's the road runs south along the coast and Belval Cove, Gibraltar and a martello tower are all passed. The tree-lined section of the road as it approaches Archirondel is known as the Pine Walk. Near its northern end a lane leads to a reservoir constructed by the Germans. Archirondel (Le Rocher Rondel or La Rocque Rondel) with its tower (1792–4), now used as a mark for shipping, lies at the northern side of the bay called Havre de Fer, while at the southern side is La Crête Point. The next bay is Anne Port with a small rocky headland—Jeffrey's Leap—at its southern side; on the inland side of the road is the Victoria Tower.

The road then runs past Castle Green, from which excellent views may be obtained of the castle and the harbour, and then turns left sharply into Gorey (see Chapter VI). From here the road turns south-west, skirting the Royal Bay of Grouville, the prefix 'Royal' being added in 1859 by command of Queen Victoria. The road turns slightly inland and runs through Gorey Common, with Gorey Village (see Chapter VI) on its northern side. On the common are the links of the Royal Jersey Golf Club, with which the names of Henry William (Harry) Vardon (1870–1937), Edward Rivers (Ted) Ray (1877–1943) and Aubrey Boomer (1897–   ) will always be associated. Nearby are two eighteenth-century fortifications—Fort William and Fort Henry. The Grouville War Memorial is passed on the right, and down a lane on the left is the Russian Cemetery, dating from 1799–1800. Between there and La Rocque Harbour are five martello towers. La Rocque approaches to being a village, but never quite becomes one. Lobster pots and fishing nets spread out to dry were once familiar sights of the place.

The road continues west through Le Bourg and Pontac to Le Hocq, where there is yet another martello tower and St. Clement's Parish Hall, which was opened in 1971. The bay to the west of the Tower is called Le Havre des Fontaines, at its western end being a headland where stands the Witches' Rock, so named because legend says that a coven of witches once used it for a meeting place. After leaving Le Hocq the road leads to Green Island and continues with Le Marais Estate to the north and La Mare Common, bordering the sea wall, to the south. It then proceeds by the coast along Grève d'Azette, with its lighthouse, and at Millard's Corner turns slightly away from the coast and continues through a more built-up area, passing on its south the Victor Hugo Hotel, incorporating No 3 Marine Terrace, where Victor Hugo lived from 1852–5, his bedroom being that now numbered 21 on the second floor. The hotel is now closed.

A short distance farther on the road leaves St. Clement, passes through a narrow strip of St. Saviour and then reaches St. Helier at Havre des Pas. On the rock called Le Rocher des Proscrits, just by the slipway at Dicq Corner, is an inscription commemorating Victor Hugo's exile in Jersey. The road then proceeds through Havre des Pas—where there is an open-air sea-water swimming-pool connected to the mainland by a bridge—and climbs up the steep hill known as Mount Bingham, so named after a former lieutenant-governor. On the right, part of the way up the hill, is Bramerton House, where T. E. Lawrence, better known as Lawrence of Arabia, stayed (1891–2) when a young child; it was there that his brother F. Helier Lawrence was born. The Lawrence family also visited Jersey in 1907, 1908 and 1909.

On the left, at the top of the hill, is La Collette House, originally the Engineers' Barracks and the lieutenant-governor's office until 1974. To the south, just short of Pointe des Pas, stands the Victoria Tower (1788), and to the south-west an electricity power station. The views from the top of Mount Bingham are extremely fine: to the east may be seen Havre des Pas and the flat coastal plain beyond, fringed by Grève d'Azette and St. Clement's Bay, while to the west is St. Helier's Harbour, then the crescent of St. Aubin's Bay and, in the far distance, Noirmont headland. There is a walk for pedestrians along the sea front from Fort d'Auvergne Hotel at Havre des Pas right around to the western entrance of the electricity power station which for part of the way is flanked on the landward side by La Collette Gardens. From Mount Bingham the road descends to the harbour, which it borders all the way into the town of St. Helier.

As late as the eighteenth century the countryside of Jersey remained entirely unspoilt. What buildings there were scattered throughout the land were built for the most part of stone and roofed with either thatch, pantiles or slates. No major roads existed, but merely a large number of lanes and tracks—many of them winding—whose routes had been laid down by immemorial usage. Orchards were to be found in great profusion. In spring the blossom-laden boughs of myriads of flowering apple trees and pear trees garlanded the land. The valleys were watered by numerous streams, working a large number of watermills. There were two towns—St. Helier, still very small, and St. Aubin, little more than a village. In the nineteenth century tremendous development took place, particularly in St. Helier, Gorey and Gorey Village, and, to a much lesser degree, throughout the island. It has, however, been since 1918, and even more so since 1945, that the greatest changes have taken place. The countryside has suffered and will suffer more, though at present the island remains, in part at least, very beautiful.

Although small in extent, Jersey's countryside is well varied, and this adds to its attractiveness. The flat coastal area of St. Clement and Grouville is quite different from the interior of the country. The wooded valleys, such as Waterworks and St. Peter's, are in complete contrast to the bleak area, comprised largely of sand-dunes and sandhills, bordering St. Ouen's Bay. The drystone walls of St. Ouen are in equally sharp contrast to the lush lanes of, say, St. Lawrence. Similarly, the deep, tree-arched lanes still to be found in the interior are in contrast to the bareness of Noirmont headland and Les Landes. The fine cliff scenery of the north, south-west and east is completely different from parts of the coastal areas of the west, south and south-east.

The valleys are small but numerous, the main ones being Val de la Mare, the upper part of which has been dammed for a reservoir; St. Peter's Valley, which, ultimately, opens out into Goose Green Marsh, Beaumont; St. Lawrence's Valley, better known as Waterworks Valley, containing a series of reservoirs—Handois (on the site of old china quarries), Dannemarche and Millbrook—reaches the sea at Millbrook; Bellozanne Valley, now visually ruined by a sewerage disposal plant and huge coal depot; Vallée des Vaux, and Grands Vaux with its reservoir, both to the north of the town; Queen's Valley, running south from St. Saviour's Hospital (the mental hospital, opened 1869); Rozel Valley; Mourier Valley; and Grève de Lecq Valley.

The Jersey New Waterworks Co. Ltd. is to be praised for the splendid way in which the reservoirs are kept; rather than detract from the beauty of the valleys in which they are situated they enhance the surroundings. Owing to its limited size the country-side does not possess those long-distant views to be found in England; occasionally one may be obtained—for instance going towards Gorey down Grouville Hill—but this is unusual. The fields are small, and each has its own name. Some of these names are commonplace, e.g. Le Grand Clos, Le Petit Clos, Le Clos de Devant; others are of interest as they provide evidence of buildings long since demolished and other pieces of information useful to the historian.

Land on a steep slope is referred to as a *côtil*. Sometimes very steep land is cultivated and *côtils* with a southern aspect are often planted with potatoes to yield early crops, but it is becoming increasingly hard to find labour to dig these *côtils*. In summer rows of tomato plants with their bamboo sticks or wooden crosses are a feature of the countryside and are to Jersey what the vines are to the wine-producing districts of France. The fields are generally divided by hedges—in the past often of thorn—and planted with trees. On the whole, trees are not well-cared for and are subjected to severe lopping with the object of obtaining maximum light for the crops. A distinguished Jersey artist, Edmund Blampied (1886–1966), in his pictures of Jersey placed on record for all time these mutilated specimens which are such a feature of the countryside.

The lanes, most of which have old French names, are narrow, winding and bordered by high hedges, often being overhung with trees which meet overhead like an arch; an example *par excellence* of such a thoroughfare was Vinchelez Lane, St. Ouen. Happily some of these Jersey lanes canopied with trees still survive. In many country lanes may be seen road scrapings, known as *bannelais*, heaped up by the hedges, these heaps being auctioned annually at a parish meeting. Ancient parish churches surrounded by their churchyards, usually with a cluster of houses, a few shops, and a public house or two, are features of the countryside, as are the nonconformist chapels, manor houses, farmhouses—some of the latter like small fortresses—and cottages. Miles of high stone walls can still be seen, although there are not as many as formerly. Property on the whole is well-cared for and gardens beautifully kept.

The face of the countryside is changing rapidly, and mixed farms are fast disappearing; in their stead are farms or holdings specializing in growing potatoes, tomatoes, broccoli (the winter cauliflower) and flowers, or a combination of these, while the number of glasshouses has increased considerably since 1945 and continues to do so. The beautiful Jersey cattle, almost deer-like in appearance, are still in evidence; sometimes they are tethered, though not as much as formerly, and in winter are to be seen wearing covers or 'coats' as they are sometimes called. The horse, that noble beast which has served Man for so long, has disappeared almost entirely from the country scene, together with the Jersey van, boxcarts, the Jersey sun bonnet, the Jersey (or Great Cow) cabbage, and so much else. The tourist industry is making its mark on the face of the countryside and hotels and guest-houses appear in the most unexpected places.

The German Underground Hospital, St. Peter's Valley. Built by the German Todt Organization during the Occupation, the hospital is hewn out of solid rock and covers four acres. It took two and a half years to construct and was fully equipped at the time of the Liberation in 1945. Never used for its intended purpose, the hospital is now preserved as a relic of the Occupation and is open to the public.

Government House, St. Saviour. Originally, the governors lived at Gorey Castle, and when that fortress was superseded by Elizabeth Castle the latter became the official residence. The next official residence was Government House in King Street, St. Helier. In 1781, however, Major Moses Corbet, the lieutenant-governor, was living at Le Manoir de la Motte in St. Helier and this was later referred to as 'Old Government House'. In 1823 the British Government exchanged the King Street residence for 'Belmont', a property situated on St. Saviour's Hill. Since that time it has been the residence of the governor or lieutenant-governor, as the case may be. The building was enlarged in 1851. There is a guardhouse or lodge at the entrance to the main gate where a sentry was mounted when a garrison was stationed in the island. Within the grounds is the lieutenant-governor's office (1974).

La Hougue Bie, Grouville. This property belongs to the Société Jersiaise (the local historical society—see Chapter VI). The word 'Hougue' refers to the splendid dolmen which stands there dating from between 3000 and 2500 B.C. The mound rises high over the dolmen and is surmounted by two ancient chapels, one with a crypt. The tomb can be entered, but a visitor must bend low to avoid hitting his head against the stone roof of the entrance passage, though it is possible to stand upright in the main chamber, which is roofed with huge blocks of granite. Giving off the main chamber are two burial chambers—one to the north and one to the south. Some of the stones used in building the dolmen came from Mont Mado, St. John, where quarrying was carried on well into the present century, and in the northern burial chamber there are numerous cup marks on two of the stones. A tower or gazebo once stood above the chapels on the mound, but this was demolished and the chapels restored (1924–5) by the Société Jersiaise. When the property belonged to Philip d'Auvergne, Duke of Bouillon, and sported its gazebo, it was known as Prince's Tower, by which name it is still occasionally referred to by the older generation. The old Jersey well-head near the entrance to the tomb was reconstructed in 1927 and was removed from 'L'Ancienneté', St. Brelade. In the grounds are a German bunker built there during the Occupation and converted (1948) into a museum containing exhibits relating to that period of the island's history, an agricultural museum (1956) containing old farm implements and carts and the horse-drawn, manually-operated fire engine formerly kept at St. Aubin, and a Jersey Eastern Railway carriage (restored 1973).

Other Archæological Sites. A number of these fall into various categories, such as habitation sites, passage graves, cists and standing stones called menhirs; in addition, there are some items which may be listed as 'miscellaneous'. The best-known dolmens are—Mont Ubé, St. Clement, lacking its capstones; Faldouet, retaining one huge capstone, and Le Couperon 're-stored', both in St. Martin; La Hougue Bie (already mentioned) at Grouville; Ville-ès-Nouaux, consisting of a long cist (a form of stone burial chamber) and another cist within a circle, at First Tower, St. Helier; the Beehive Hut, so called because of its conical shape, at La Sergenté, St. Brelade; and Les Monts Grantez, St. Ouen.

In addition, there are eight menhirs, namely: La Dame Blanche, Blanche Pierre or Ivy Stone, off Samarès Lane, St. Clement; the Great Menhir in the Upper Quennevais; the Little Menhir and the Broken Menhir in the Lower Quennevais; Les Trois Rocques, near St. Ouen's Pond, and the White Menhir, 200 yards south of Les Trois Rocques. Just by the platform of the old railway station at Corbière is a rectangular block of granite called La Table des Marthes, under which prehistoric objects were found.

There is also an ancient stone (a block of red granite) called La Pierre des Baissières, situated nearly opposite the entrance to the Roman Catholic Church of St. Matthieu at the point where the parishes of St. Lawrence, St. Mary and St. Peter meet, and on which cup marks appear. La Cotte à la Chèvre and La Cotte de St. Brelade are two cave dwellings, the latter being a site of first-class importance still undergoing excavation.

St. Peter's Bunker Museum of German Equipment and Occupation Relics is situated opposite St. Peter's Church. It occupies a German-built bunker and contains numerous well-displayed exhibits relating to the Occupation. Nearby is the *Jersey Motor Museum*.

The Zoo, Les Augrès, Trinity. Founded by Gerald Durrell in 1959, it was opened to the public at Easter of that year and has since become the headquarters of The Jersey Wildlife Preservation Trust of Jersey, formed in 1963. A collection of animals and birds has already been built up and is being steadily increased. The house and its outbuildings are old and very attractive. One of the archways bears the Arms of thé Dumaresqs, and there are a number of dated stones about the property.

The Ecréhous and the Minquiers. The Ecréhous are a reef of islets and rocks lying off the north-east coast of Jersey, approximately half-way between the island and France, and are considered to be part of the parish of St. Martin. The three main islets are Maître Ile, Marmotière and Blanc Ile. They were inhabited in pre-historic times, but the first mention of them in historic times does not occur until 1203. A few houses and cottages have been built on the Ecréhous, on Maître Ile are the ruins of a priory, and on Marmotière there is a Customs House displaying the Arms of Jersey. In the nineteenth century Philip Pinel, a Jerseyman, lived there for many years and as a result was nicknamed 'King of the Ecréhous'.

The Minquiers are a reef of islets and rocks covering a large area lying to the south of St. Helier, less than half-way between Jersey and France. They were inhabited in prehistoric times. In the past considerable quantities of stone were quarried there. On the principal islet, Maîtresse Ile, there is a Customs House and a few other buildings, but there are no buildings on the second islet of the group, Les Maisons. The Minquiers are considered part of the parish of Grouville. During the German occupation the occupying forces stationed an anti-aircraft battery on the reef.

Living Things. Although Jersey is becoming increasingly urbanized, wild life does still exist; but the Island's double-horned sheep and the red-legged partridge—the latter found in such numbers that it was nicknamed 'Jerseyman'—are both now extinct. It is said that the last red-legged partridge to be seen locally was shot at Plémont in 1876. The hare has also become extinct, but the stoat and rabbit are still found, as are also the frog, newt and toad. The latter, named 'Le Crapaud', used to grow to a great size and was very numerous, so much so that 'Crapaud' became the nickname for a Jerseyman—there was even once a newspaper of that name. Lizards, both the green and wall varieties, are to be found in Jersey, as are the grass snake and the humble slow-worm. The lizards are very attractive little creatures and may be seen basking in the sunshine on warm summer days. There are also voles, including the Jersey Bank Vole, brown rats and black rats, long-tailed field mice and common house mice, hedgehogs, shrews (including a Jersey variety), moles, bats and red squirrels.

There is also much in Jersey to interest the botanist, and the Société Jersiaise has a small but active Botanical Section. Unfortunately, as the island becomes more built over so the wild plants are destroyed, but thankfully it may be said that bluebells, wild daffodils and primroses still survive, together with bulrushes, wild irises, bracken, gorse and heather. Jersey specialities are the minute Jersey or Sand Crocus, the Jersey Orchid and the Jersey Fern (also found in Guernsey). The Belladonna Lily (*Amaryllis belladonna*) is grown in quite a large number of gardens and is sometimes referred to as the Jersey Lily.

II

FACE OF THE ISLANDS—II

... thou Guernsey! bravely crowned!
With rough embattled rocks, whose venom hating ground
The harden'd emeril hath, which thou abroad dost send;
Thou Ligou, her beloved, and Sark, that doth attend
Her pleasure every hour, as Jethou, them at need,
With pheasants, fallow deer, and conies thou dost feed! ...

Michael Drayton

The Bailiwick of Guernsey comprises the islands of Guernsey, Alderney, Sark, Herm and Jethou, as well as certain other islets and rocks in the vicinity. Guernsey is the most westerly of the Channel Islands and consequently the farthest away from France; it has an area of twenty-four square miles and slopes from south to north away from the sun. The prevailing wind is south-west; at certain times, however, it blows steadily from the east. As in the case of Jersey, the Gulf Stream makes the Island's climate milder than it would otherwise be, but the air is more bracing. As in the sister island, snow rarely settles for any length of time. Guernsey is divided into ten parishes, namely: Castel (otherwise spelt Câtel), Forest, St. Andrew's, St. Martin's, St. Peter-in-the-Wood, St. Peter Port, St. Sampson's, St. Saviour's, Torteval and Vale. With the exception of St. Andrew's, each parish borders the sea; St. Martin's is divided into two by Forest, St. Sampson's is similarly divided by Vale, and Torteval by St. Peter-in-the-Wood.

The island has many good bays, notably on the east coast to the south of St. Peter Port—Soldiers' Bay and Fermain Bay; along the south coast from east to west are Petit Port, Moulin Huet, Saints, Petit Bôt and Portelet; on the west coast from south to north are Rocquaine, L'Erée, Vazon, Cobo, Grandes Rocques, Port Soif, Portinfer and Chouet; on the north are Pembroke Bay

A traditional Jersey lane

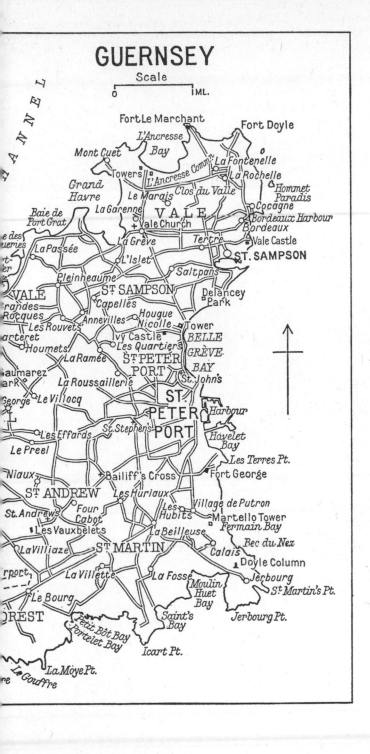

GUERNSEY

Scale

0   1 ML.

tower. On the headland on the north side of the bay is a curious little round white-washed building known either as the Cockle (Le Coquelin) or the Pepper Pot, which was erected during the Napoleonic Wars as a shelter for the guard. There is only room inside for one man standing up. In summer there is a boat service between the Albert Pier at St. Peter Port harbour and Fermain Bay.

Returning to Village de Putron, the road then proceeds past the gates of Sausmarez Manor (see Chapter VIII) to the St. Martin's War Memorial, where on the left is the Jerbourg Road leading to the Doyle Column, St. Martin's Point and Jerbourg Point. The column was erected to the memory of Sir John Doyle, Bt., K.B., Lieutenant-Governor of Guernsey (1803–16), who held the office with distinction and was to that island what General Sir George Don was to Jersey. The column, destroyed during the German Occupation, was replaced by the present one in 1953. On the coast to the east lies a little pine wood above Divette with Pied du Mur (Marble Bay) and the small headland of Bec du Nez beyond. At St. Martin's Point is a lighthouse, reached by means of a bridge. Immediately to the west of the point is Vaux Bêtes (Telegraph Bay). At Jerbourg are traces of ancient earthworks, and from the south-west tip of the point there is a good view of the Pea Stacks, a group of rocks to the south, and of Moulin Huet Bay, Saints Bay and Icart Point to the west.

From Jerbourg, too, it is possible to walk westward along the cliffs, keeping the attractive coastline and the sea constantly in view. The motorist has several alternative routes to the west and is able either to return to the St. Martin's War Memorial and then proceed by way of La Beilleuse through the districts of Mouilpied, La Valette and Le Bourg, past the airport, or to take several of a number of smaller roads, which will more or less bring him to the same spot. The main road divides just about midway along the south side of the airport, the southern fork proceeding close to Torteval Church, the tower and spire of which look as if they have escaped from an illustration in a book of fairy-tales.

Along the coast between Jerbourg Point and Icart Point to the west are a number of delightful bays and coves—Petit Port, with its lovely sands; Moulin Huet, with the Cradle Rock and the Dog and Lion Rocks a short distance offshore, the latter looking very much like the animals after which they are named; Bon Port and Saints Bay, where are to be found a martello tower, a small harbour (Le Havre de Blanchelande) and a battery. To the south-west of Saints Bay are Icart and Icart Point, from which there are splendid views both east and west.

Continuing westward along the coast, four bays—La Bette, Le Jaonnet, Petit Bôt and Portelet—and the little cove called Les Sommeillcuses are passed before one reaches La Moye Point, which stands almost in a direct line with Icart Point. A little way beyond the point is Le Gouffre, a small, steep valley opening on to the seashore, and, still going westward, is La Corbière Point, with Havre de Bon Repos and Venus Pool just beyond. Standing slightly back from the cliff, a little to the west, is a tower built by the Germans during the Occupation on the site of the old Prévôté Watch House. Further along the coast are Les Ecrilleurs and a number of other inlets and indentations in the cliffs too numerous to mention, until Pleinmont is reached, which promontory forms the south-west corner of the island. One feature of this coastline which must be referred to is Le Souffleur, a blow-hole reputed to be the best in the Channel Islands and situated in the Baie de la Forge below Mont Hérault.

From Pleinmont Point, with its television masts and beautiful wild scenery, a good view is obtained of the Hanois Lighthouse standing a mile and a quarter out to sea on Le Biseau Rock; built by Trinity House, it rises 117 feet above its base and was first lit in 1862. At the north-west tip of the headland stands Fort Pezeries, and just offshore is the Compass Rock. Close to the sea on the north side of the headland is La Table des Pions, a small circular piece of turf surrounded by a trench with stones bounding the outer circumference; *pions* (footmen) who took part in the old ceremony of La Chevauchée de St. Michel (see Chapter XIV) used the patch of turf as a table around which they sat with their legs in the trench.

To the east of La Table des Pions is Portelet Harbour with its small jetty. Looking northward, the whole expanse of Rocquaine Bay—the largest in Guernsey—may be seen with the Island of Lihou in the far distance. The west coast from here to L'Ancresse, washed by the waters of the Atlantic, is rocky and interspersed with good sandy beaches, the rather desolate coastal plain being protected from the inroads of the sea by a strong wall. The main

road skirts the bay and passes Fort Grey (or Château de Rocquaine), a small fortification situated on an eminence just off the
shore at the end of a short causeway.

At the northern extremity of Rocquaine Bay is L'Erée, where
stands a tall martello tower called Fort Saumarez. Nearby a
causeway leads to the Island of Lihou, which has an area of about
50 acres and is one-third of a mile long. It contains little of
interest beyond the remains of the ancient Priory of Our Lady
of Lihou. The priory is known to have been in existence as long
ago as 1156; its total length was about 68 feet, the nave being
about 23 feet wide and the chancel about 20 feet. A carved stone
let into the wall of 'Bon Air', a house at Les Adams, St. Peter's, is
supposed to depict the priory and has an inscription which
includes the date 1114. The newly constructed dwelling on Lihou
is occupied by a caretaker.

Returning to the mainland, the main road continues to follow
the coast along Perelle Bay until Fort Richmond is reached. Less
than a mile inland is St. Saviour's Reservoir, built between 1938
and 1947. The work was held up during the Occupation, hence
the delay in completion. The reservoir is capable of holding
240,000,000 gallons of water and of supplying 2,000,000 gallons a
day. The dam, 900 feet in length, is built across the main St.
Saviour's Valley north of where it joins two side valleys—Les
Choffins to the east and Les Padins to the west.

From Perelle Bay the coast road turns eastward and cuts across
the neck of a small peninsula—Le Crocq, where a house named
Fort Le Crocq is built on the site of a former fortification. Beyond
Le Crocq the road skirts Vazon Bay where Fort Houmet, dating
from the nineteenth century, stands on a promontory at its
northern end.

The main road skirts Cobo Bay and then proceeds past Saline
Bay, from where it goes slightly inland before rejoining the coast
at Port Soif. It then goes past Portinfer, Baie des Pequèries, Baie
de Pulias and Baie de Port Grat until Grand Havre is reached.
Grand Havre is a large inlet at what used to be the western end of
La Braye du Valle, a shallow stretch of water once dividing the
northern extremity of the island from the remainder. The road
just before Vale Church is named Pont St. Michel, recalling the
existence of the Braye. Near Vale Church once stood the Priory
of St. Michael of the Vale, the remains of which were demolished

in 1928, but still existing to the north is the ancient *garenne* or warren of the Fief of Anneville, surrounded by a dry ditch.

The main road as it goes northward keeps away from the coast, passing La Garenne and Baie des Grèves on the left, and when it reaches the eighteen-hole golf links at L'Ancresse it turns right. At this point a side road runs north-west to Chouet and Mont Cuet, while another runs north to Pembroke Bay at the western end of L'Ancresse Bay, where Fort Pembroke stands to the west and Fort Le Marchant to the east. L'Ancresse Common stretches across the whole of the northern end of the island, the area being open heathland covered with furze and gorse—and martello towers.

The main road passing to the south of the golf course is called Les Clôtures Road, and as it goes eastward it changes its name to Les Mielles Road; at La Fontenelle it bears to the south-east through the district of La Rochelle. To the north-east lie Fontenelle Bay, Banque au Mouton, Fort Doyle (dating from the nineteenth century), Fontaine ès Boeufs and Miellette Bay.

The road then turns south through the district of Cocagne. A short distance off the coast are the islets known as Hommet Paradis and Hommet Benest. Bordeaux and its harbour are next reached, and from there the coast road keeps close to the shore and curves westward, keeping Vale Castle (see Chapter VII) to its right and proceeds through the town of St. Sampson (see Chapter VII) on towards St. Peter Port.

The district of Saltpans lying to the west of the town of St. Sampson takes its name from saltpans once found there, but distinct from the saltpans were the saltings, low-lying fields of coarse grass, which in the days when La Braye du Valle existed were covered at times by the sea and when dry were used for grazing.

A side road runs along the south side of St. Sampson's Harbour and turns right into Bulwer Avenue, which passes close by the shore and rejoins the main road at Richmond Corner. The coast road then follows the line of Belle Grève Bay, passing on the right the Château des Marais or Ivy Castle (see Chapter VIII), into the outskirts of St. Peter Port.

As was the case with Jersey, Guernsey remained entirely unspoilt until the eighteenth century, and the types of buildings then existing were the same as those on the sister island, and, similarly, there were few roads. Guernsey at that time had only one town—St. Peter Port—which was still very small. In the nineteenth century tremendous development took place in the island: St. Peter Port was greatly enlarged, La Braye du Valle drained, and a new town, St. Sampson, was built. As the century advanced buildings spread, but it is during the twentieth century that the greatest changes have occurred. The island is now largely built over with houses and glasshouses, the latter being very noticeable from the air.

As with Jersey, the Guernsey countryside is varied, but being more built over there is less unspoilt inland scenery. The bleak coastal scenery of the west is in sharp contrast to the cliff scenery of the south and south-east, as is L'Ancresse Common with some of the rural areas more towards the south. The valleys are smaller than in Jersey, but some of them, such as Moulin Huet and Petit Bôt, are very beautiful, and long-distant views are only occasionally obtained.

As tomato plants growing in open fields are typical of Jersey's countryside in summer, so glasshouses are typical of Guernsey's. Each field has a name. Trees are more scarce than they are in the sister island. The roads and lanes are narrow and in rural areas are bordered by high hedges which sometimes incorporate drystone work.

Le Déhus Dolmen and Other Archæological Sites. Le Déhus is the name of a fine large passage grave situated at Paradis, Vale, belonging to the States and under the care of the Ancient Monuments Committee. It was first excavated in 1837 by Frederick Corbin Lucas, an eminent Guernsey antiquary who was responsible for many archæological excavations in the island. The tomb was re-excavated on behalf of the States in 1932, and after reconstruction it was re-opened to the public in the following year. A feature of interest is the guardian of the tomb, a figure wearing a one-edged short sword, carved on the underside of the second capstone of the main chamber.

Other archæological sites are at L'Erée, St. Peter's, where there is a passage grave called Le Creux ès Faies; at Delancey Park, St. Sampson's, are the remains of a megalithic structure; at the Catioroc, St. Saviour's, is a passage grave—Le Trépied Dolmen—in times gone by a regular meeting place for witches and referred to in a number of witch trials; in the Vale there are two more and covers an area of some 400 acres. It is a delightful place, and anyone seeing the shell beach with the sun shining and the sea a vivid blue might well imagine that they were in some far-away place—even a tropical island.

The harbour with its old crane lies on the west of the island, facing St. Peter Port. At its head is a group of buildings constituting the island's 'village', and comprising a hotel, café, shop and a few other buildings. Near the hotel is a tennis court by which stands what is reputed to be the smallest prison in the Channel Islands—if not in the world—dating from about 1826; built of granite and circular in shape, it has a diameter of 13 feet 6 inches with a roof like a bee-skep and without a window.

Tracks and footpaths lead from the harbour to all parts of the island, one going northward along the coast passes the old cemetery on the left and skirts Le Monteau (Monk's Hill) on the right. After turning inland it again runs north with a hillock to the east and another to the north-west—Le Grand Monteau and Le Petit Monteau. The track divides as it reaches the Common, beyond which Mousonnière Bay stretches along the whole length of the island's northern coast. On the beach embedded in the sand is an ancient burial chamber, while a small obelisk—La Pierre aux Rats—built by Jonathan Duncan, author of the well-known *History of Guernsey* (1841), on the site of 'La Longue Pierre', stands on the Common a little inland from the centre of the bay. Part of the Common has been laid out as a golf course. At the northern end of the island's east coast is the famous beach composed of a myriad of minute shells. A little way along the coast to the south is Belvoir Bay with a fine sandy beach. The remainder of the island's coastline on the east, south and west as far as the harbour consists of low cliffs. There is a large cave called Le Creux du Pignon in the southern cliffs near Pointe de Sauzebourge. A second landing-place, Rosière Steps, is situated a short distance to the south of the harbour.

In the centre of the island stands the Manor House, once described by Sir Compton Mackenzie, who was the tenant from 1920 to 1923, as "the ugliest building in Europe". Services are held regularly in the nearby ancient chapel of St. Tugual with its separate bell tower. As in the case of its smaller neighbour, Jethou, there are no buses or cars on Herm, and the island remains unspoilt, despite the large number of people who visit it. Many

interesting wild flowers are to be found as well as a large population of rabbits. Wallabies were introduced by Prince Blücher
von Wahlstatt (great grandson of the Field-Marshal) when he
was the tenant, but, unfortunately, although they bred none has
survived.

Between Herm and the neighbouring island of Jethou, lying
to the west, are two rocks, one of which is called La Pierre
Percée because of the artificial hole which has been made through
it, and to the north of this rock is the other—L'Hermitier—
accessible from Herm at low tide by a causeway. On the east side
of the island and to the south of Belvoir Bay are two more rocks
—Caquorobert and Putrainée.

Tourism and dairy farming are the sources of income of this
small, but delightful island.

Jethou

Jethou lies three miles out from St. Peter Port in the direction of
Herm. It is a circular hump of land with a flat top and has an area
of about 20 acres and a circumference of about $1\frac{1}{4}$ miles, with offshore islets—Crevichon to the north, Petite Fauconnière and
Grande Fauconnière to the south. From the boat-house, where
passengers from Guernsey are discharged, a path runs westward
past the café and gift shop in the direction of the Manor, the
residence of the tenant. Sir Compton Mackenzie lived there when
he was tenant of the island (1920–34). The present house is a
successor of an earlier one known to have been in existence as
long ago as 1710. Behind the garden with its very old mulberry
tree is the small and delightful Manor Wood. Flowers for export
are grown in the island's few fields. On the east coast is a raised
beach and to the north of Fauconnière Bay is a *creux* or blow-hole,
known as the Devil's Hole.

Alderney

> ... Thou fruitful Aurency, near to the ancient Celtic shore,
> To Ushant and the Seams, whereas those nuns of yore
> Gave answers from their caves, and took what shapes they please,
> Ye happy islands set within the British seas.
>
> Michael Drayton

Alderney is the third largest and most northerly of the Channel thousands, principally puffins, although gulls, oyster-catchers, razor-bills, shags and stormy petrels are also to be found—not to mention rabbits. The States of Alderney maintain a hut on the island which can be hired for a small fee. Just off Burhou is an even smaller islet called Little Burhou. It is a strange fact that the flora of the two islands are largely different. On Ortac, a neighbouring rock, there is a colony of gannets.

The Casquets. This is a dangerous reef of rocks about a mile and a half in length and about half a mile across. The northern rock is conical in shape and on it stands the lighthouse. Originally there were three lighthouses—St. Peter, St. Thomas and the Donjon, but when Trinity House assumed responsibility for them in 1877 the two latter were abolished and the third improved.

Sark

> Sark, fairer than aught in the world that the lit skies cover,
> Laughs inly behind her cliffs, and the sea-farers mark
> As a shrine where the sunlight serves, though the blown clouds
> hover,
> Sark.
>
> A. C. Swinburne (1837–1909)

Sark lies $7\frac{1}{2}$ miles to the east of Guernsey. The island stands high out of the sea to an average height of 300 feet and is about $3\frac{1}{2}$ miles from north to south and a mile and a half at its widest point. It consists of two parts, the larger Great Sark, and the smaller Little Sark, connected by a narrow isthmus—La Coupée. Included with Sark is the Island of Brechou, which lies off the western tip of Great Sark.

This delightful island of Sark is approached by sea, the landing generally being made at La Mascline Harbour (1938–49), which has almost entirely superseded the neighbouring old harbour of Le Creux. The latter was started possibly by Helier de Carteret (*c.* 1532–*c.* 1581), the first Seigneur, but more probably by his son, Sir Philip de Carteret. The new harbour was opened by H.R.H. the Duke of Edinburgh in 1949; it is overlooked by the lighthouse (1912) at Point Robert, built of blue granite quarried from L'Eperquerie Common. Both harbours are reached through tunnels. The first of the two to Le Creux was cut in 1588; the second in 1866.

Harbour Hill winds up from the harbours to the plateau above. As there are no cars or buses on the island the only way to reach the top is by horse-carriage, obtaining a lift on a tractor trailer, or on foot; the gradient is steep and the walker should take it slowly. A cliff path to the left leads past Les Lâches, with its anchorage for fishing boats, beyond which are Petite Derrible Bay and Derrible Bay, where is the splendid Creux Derrible measuring 80 feet across and 180 feet deep.

At Aval du Creux, near the top of the Harbour Hill, is Sark's granite-built power station (1954), and a little further on the crossroads at La Collinette are reached. Here a turning to the right known as La Rue Lucas goes northwards to Le Carrefour and La Rue du Fort, which leads to the settlement of Le Fort, with La Banquette Landing, reached by a path, to the east. A road to the right off La Rue Lucas leads to the lighthouse at Point Robert. On the way it passes the Mermaid Tavern, and just beyond turns sharply to the left and then as sharply to the right, where a track runs northwards narrowing into a path as it zig-zags down into the bay called La Grève de la Ville, with its natural arch called La Chapelle des Mauves.

Southwards from La Collinette runs a road which soon branches in three different directions, west to D'Icart and Le Dixcart de Haut, south to Le Petit Dixcart, Baker's Valley and Dixcart Bay, the latter divided from Derrible Bay by the headland known as the Hog's Back, and east to La Forge. Westwards from La Collinette lies the Avenue, a continuation of the Harbour Hill, which was originally the driveway of Le Manoir, and until the Occupation was lined with trees. Here are to be found most of the island's shops and two banks (one with a clock tower which is illuminated at night). Towards the western end of the Avenue is a house, formerly the arsenal of the Sark Militia, which was disbanded in 1880, and beyond stands the tiny barrel-roofed prison dated 1856, containing only two cells. A turning to the right, La Chasse Marais, leads to St. Peter's Church (see Chapter VIII), the Boys' School (where meetings of the Chief Pleas are held—see Chapter V), and the Recreation Hall. The road runs northwards with La Seigneurie (see Chapter VIII) and its lovely garden (open to the public on Mondays) on the left and continues until it reaches L'Eperquerie Common and then, reduced first to a track and then to a path, attains the northern tip of the island. In the

The Royal Square, St. Helier, Jersey

grounds of La Seigneurie is a small brass cannon, with an inscription in French stating that it was a gift by Queen Elizabeth I to Helier de Carteret in 1572, which was one of a number of pieces of ordnance sent to him from the Tower of London. The cannons in various places on the cliffs are fired on special occasions and are of more recent date. Near La Seigneurie is a house named 'La Moinerie', recalling the time, long centuries ago, when monks lived on Sark.

Below the eastern side of the Common is Les Fontaines Bay with two natural rock arches—the Twin Sisters or Fairies' Grotto. North of the bay is L'Eperquerie Landing and still further Bec du Nez, the most northern tip of the island. Around the coast to the west are the Boutiques Caves, inaccessible except at low tide, while further to the south is Saignie Bay and the group of rocks called Les Autelets at Port du Moulin.

Returning to La Seigneurie, a road runs westwards to Port du Moulin, passing on the left an attractive old property, L'Ecluse (now a small hotel), where there is a dam that was used by the monks. A cliff path leads down to Port du Moulin where there is an artificial square opening in the rock named 'The Window' with a sheer drop of 250 feet to the sea. This opening was made for the purpose of hauling up goods from below. To the south-west from Port du Moulin opposite Gouliot Headland, Gouliot Caves and Moie de Gouliot, across the narrow Gouliot Passage, is Brechou Island. While still further to the south lies Havre Gosselin named after Nicholas Gosselin, a friend of Helier de Carteret, who helped him to obtain the concession of Sark in 1563. Nearby is the Pilcher Monument (1868), erected to the memory of a Mr. Pilcher and his companions, who were drowned when their small sailing boat sank during a squall. A road runs inland from Havre Gosselin, passing the duck pond (see Chapter XIV) next to Petit Beauregard farmhouse, to the crossroads at La Vaurocque, to the west of which is the windmill (see Chapter VIII) standing 375 feet above sea level. The main road goes south from the crossroads over La Coupée to Little Sark, with a turning on the left, about half-way between the crossroads and La Coupée, leading to Dixcart Bay, and a track on the right, leading to the Tenement of Dos d'Ane beyond which at the foot of the cliffs is Port ès Saies.

The road across La Coupée, a spectacular isthmus, 100 yards

long and 300 feet high—"one sheer thread of narrowing preci-
pice"—with a sheer drop on both sides, connects the two parts of
Sark. La Coupée was the subject of a drawing by J. M. W.
Turner. To the west lies Grande Grève, the island's largest and
most sandy bay, accessible from La Coupée by a path and steps;
to the east Convanche Bay with Convanche Chasm at its northern
side, large enough in calm weather to row a boat through, and the
Lamentation Caves at its southern side, so called because of the
moaning sound emitted by them at certain states of the tide.

The road continues southwards through Little Sark (a turning
to the left leads to Creux Pot), passes the tower of another old
windmill on the right, and finally divides at La Sablonnerie, one
fork going west to the Tenements of Pipeterie, Du Val and Du
Vallerie, and the other east to the Barracks, with paths leading to
the silver mines, Port Gorey and Venus Pool. In Pot Bay is Le
Pot, one of Sark's famous creux. Off the south tip of Little Sark
are the horseshoe-shaped Venus Pool and the Jupiter Pool, two
natural depressions in the rocks. Lying a quarter of a mile off the
south tip of the island is the large islet called L'Etac, where
puffins are often to be seen. On the western side of Little Sark is
Port Gorey, an inlet in the cliffs, above which are the remains of
the Sark silver mines, and along the coast to the north is another
natural indentation in the rocks—Adonis Pool, which is larger
than the Venus Pool already mentioned.

Brechou—otherwise known as Ile des Marchands after its one
time owners—is approximately 1,000 yards from east to west and
500 yards from north to south; it lies to the west of Great Sark
across the Gouillot Passage and has two landing places, one of
which—Le Port—is on its western side and is never used. A
mansion and a number of smaller dwellings have been built on
the island, which is one of the tenements whose owner has a seat
in the Chief Pleas.

Sark is a truly beautiful island, especially in springtime when
wild flowers bloom in profusion. Dixcart Valley presents a lovely
sight with thousands of bluebells, primroses and other wild
flowers and ferns, also the large wild rhubarb. It is not only
beautiful, however, but peaceful; except for the occasional sound
of a tractor, no man-made noise strikes harshly upon the ear and
no noxious fumes offend the nose. This silence is very marked at
dusk when it can almost be felt.

Although the Channel Islands undoubtedly possess many similarities, they are not entirely alike and are, in fact, variations on a theme, each island having its own particular atmosphere and character. The differences between the two larger islands and the smaller ones are too obvious to mention, but it is worthwhile considering the differences between Jersey and Guernsey. The former island slopes into the sun and the latter slopes away from it. The difference in size between the two is definitely noticeable, with Jersey retaining a greater area of unspoilt countryside in relation to its size than Guernsey. Jersey granite, once used extensively for building and still used to a somewhat lesser degree, tends to be pinkish, while in Guernsey the granite, also formerly in general use for building, is usually grey.

St. Helier, built principally on a low-lying flat area, is completely different from St. Peter Port, which is built on a hillside. There are also many minor points of difference between the islands—the helmets of the policemen, the colour of the telephone boxes and of the street nameplates, the livery of the buses—each small in itself but cumulatively adding up to a fairly considerable dissimilarity. It is these differences that give each island a distinct personality—coupled, of course, with the inhabitants.

Jersey, the largest of the group, stands slightly aloof from the other islands—sophisticated, bustling with life, appealing to wealthy residents and tourists, but still retaining a strong agricultural element. Guernsey, very much part of the group, maybe less sophisticated but with a more relaxed atmosphere, also bustling with life, has a strong agricultural element, some wealthy residents and fewer tourists. Alderney, windswept and bleak when the sky darkens and the winds blow and the sea is whipped into a fury, is independent, free and easy. Sark, beautiful and tranquil, away from it all, is where time seems to stand still—well almost still. And little Herm is like a South Sea island that has got lost in the Channel.

III

THE PEOPLE

> ... there still lingers a certain individuality
> about the thoroughbred Channel Islander; to the
> world in general he asserts himself an Englishman,
> but in the presence of the English he boasts of being
> a Jerseyman or a Guernseyman.
>
> Edith Carey (1864–1935)

The Channel Islands are highly populated. At the last census (1971) the Bailiwick of Jersey had a population of 72,629; and the Bailiwick of Guernsey 52,708, made up of Guernsey (50,436), Alderney (1,690), Herm and Jethou (105) and Sark and Brechou (582). The population of Jersey has increased considerably since then, and there have almost undoubtedly been increases in those of all the other islands. These increases are accounted for by immigration, which has taken place on quite a large scale, with the result that there are many non-natives now living in the islands. Such was not always the case, and until the beginning of the nineteenth century the inhabitants of the Channel Islands were predominantly, although not exclusively, of Norman descent, as they had been before 1204 when the islands formed part of the Duchy of Normandy.

Most native families can be traced back to the start of the parish registers (see Chapter VIII), and in many cases it is possible to prove from various other documentary sources that many of these families were firmly established in the islands centuries before then.

It has been estimated that in Jersey alone over 450 surnames have been known since the sixteenth century. What is noteworthy is that certain families are identified either exclusively or largely with one or other of the principal islands. For example, the surnames Ahier, Amy, Bailhache, Balleine, Baudains, Benest,

Bichard, Billot, Bisson, Blampied, Bois, Coutanche, d'Authreau, de la Mare, du Pré, Durell, Ereaut, Falle, Gallichan, Gaudin, Gibaut, Giffard, Gruchy, Hamon, Huelin, Jeune, La Cloche, Larbalestier, Le Breton, Le Brocq, Le Cornu, Le Couteur, Le Maistre, Le Marquand, Le Sauteur, Le Vavasseur dit Durell, Mourant, Noel, Orange, Picot, Pirouet, Quérée, Renouf, Simon, Sincl, Touzel and Vautier are found in Jersey; while the surnames Bréhaut, Collenette, de Jersey, de Putron, de Sausmarez, Falla, Gallienne, Jehan, Keyho, Lainé, Le Gallez, Le Huray, Le Page, Le Patourel, Le Pelley, Le Tissier, Mahy, Marquand, Mauger, Ozanne, Rabey, Robilliard and Torode are to be found in Guernsey.

The origin of the name de Sausmarez is interesting. It is first mentioned in connection with Guernsey in a letter of 1254 referring to William de Saumareis, who was probably William de Salinelles, Seigneur of Samarès, in Jersey (the de Salinelles were descended from the Norman family of St. Hilaire du Harcourt), but it is not known precisely when the de Sausmarez family first took up residence in Guernsey. The family renewed its links with Jersey when Matthew de Sausmarez married Anne Durell, daughter of John Durell and Anne Dumaresq of that island, whose portrait hangs in the dining-room of Sausmarez Manor. The Jersey connection was further strengthened when three of Matthew's daughters, Madeline, Elizabeth and Anne married Philip Durell (who rose to be a Vice-Admiral), George Durell and Philip Dumaresq, all Jerseymen.

Occasionally a predominantly Jersey name is found in Guernsey and *vice versa* and some surnames are shared by both the principal islands. Where surnames are to be found in common their pronunciation is sometimes different in each island. Two examples of such names are Langlois and Le Poidevin. It will also have been noted from the two lists of surnames that in Jersey is found that of Le Marquand, whereas in Guernsey the same surname is found without the prefix. In Jersey occurs the surname Le Masurier; in Guernsey there is a similar surname Le Mesurier. Nowadays some Jersey surnames, such as Le Marquand, Mollet and Pallot, are still pronounced in the French way, while others, such as Gaudin, Poingdestre and Voisin, in the English way. The surname du Feu is an example of a name which is pronounced in both ways. In Jersey, popular christian names were Francis, John,

Peter and Philip, although in the French form. During the nineteenth century and in the early years of the twentieth century, Garnet, Hedley, Snowdon, Wesley and Winter were popular. Certain christian names are frequently combined with particular surnames, e.g. Nicholas with Le Quesne; Philip with de Carteret.

Alderney is the most anglicized of all the islands, and a large proportion of the population bears English surnames. However, both Jersey and Guernsey surnames are also well in evidence. Barbenson, Cauvain, Duplain, Gaudion, Herivel, Le Ber, Le Cocq and Renier are surnames particularly associated with the island.

Sark is the least anglicized of the islands and consequently insular surnames predominate, notably: Carré, de Carteret, Falle Hamon, Le Feuvre, Perrée and Vibert.

Down the centuries people of many nationalities have settled in the Channel Islands, and their blood has mingled with that of the native islanders. In 1572, after the massacre of St. Bartholomew, and following the revocation of the Edict of Nantes, large numbers of French Protestants, commonly called Huguenots, fled to the islands and some of them settled there. A well-known Jersey family of Huguenot descent is that of de Faye; a well-known Guernsey one is Lainé.

On the whole, as has been said, the population remained largely unchanged. Furthermore, families tended to remain in certain districts and marry into others in the same areas. Even today, certain Jersey families are associated with particular parishes, e.g. Noel, Renouf, Richardson and Whitley with St. Martin; Arthur with St. Mary, Labey with Grouville. That is one of the reasons why the pronunciation of Jersey-French, as well as in some cases the words themselves, varies from parish to parish. It therefore follows that a person well versed in the language is able to detect the area a Jerseyman comes from by hearing him speak Jersey-French. Similar remarks apply to Guernsey, where, for example, the families of Carey, de Vic, Gosselin, Lefebvre and de Sausmarez are associated with the parish of St. Martin, and there are basically three versions of Guernsey-French—North, South and St. Martin's. It must not be assumed that because a Jerseyman or a Guernseyman, and particularly the former, has a French-sounding name that he comes of an insular family, because since 1815 a large number of French people, principally Normans and

Bretons (often originally brought over as potato diggers), have settled in the islands, more especially Jersey.

Channel Islanders spoke their respective variations of the Norman-French language—some of them still do in Jersey, Guernsey and Sark—which is similar to that still spoken by the country people of Normandy. Accepted French was reserved for Church and Chapel, the Royal Court, the States and, when they appeared, for a number of the newspapers. At one time if a Jerseyman spoke French instead of his native tongue he was considered to be a snob. English first gained a foothold in St. Helier and St. Peter Port, and ultimately general ascendancy throughout the islands in the late nineteenth century and early this century until today when it is universally used. It is pleasing to know that in each of the two larger islands there is a society devoted to the preservation of the local Norman-French. Even nowadays in Jersey, Guernsey and Sark the truly native islanders who speak the local Norman-French use it when talking to each other, and it is surprising how many retain the language; also how many have a knowledge of accepted French. Just as the natives of each county in England have their own distinctive accent, so Channel Islanders have theirs when speaking English, Jersey's varying from that of Guernsey. In the former island, at any rate, emphasis is sometimes put on the wrong syllable of a word, which produces very strange results. There is also a tendency for islanders whose native tongue is really the local Norman-French when speaking English to use phrases which are literal translations from the French.

Those people from outside the Channel Islands who have down the centuries come to settle there, have, until the present century, been largely assimilated into the local populations. However, from the nineteenth century the number of newcomers has become so large that it has no longer been possible for them to be absorbed, and with inevitable intermarriage between native islanders and immigrants (who today include Italians, Spaniards and Portuguese), coupled with gradual changes in the traditional way of life, the local characteristics of the people are fast disappearing. It is, therefore, worth noting such characteristics before they have totally disappeared and been forgotten.

It is difficult to generalize about people—even native inhabitants of small communities like those of the Channel Islands—

so consequently the limitations of anything written in the following paragraphs must be accepted.

Channel Islanders are mostly short, dark and not especially good-looking, Guernseymen tending to be of smaller stature than Jerseymen. Where looks are concerned there have been some notable exceptions, an example being the celebrated beauty Lillie Langtry, who was born in Jersey. The artist Edmund Blampied portrayed *par excellence* the physical appearance of the Jerseyman and in the same way "Ph'lp et Merienne", created by Edward Henry Le Brocq, and "Bram Bilo (Chant'nyi d'St-Ou)", created by P. Le S. Mourant, some years earlier, were characters which typified the humour and thinking of a certain section of Jersey people.

The late C. T. Le Quesne, Q.C. (1885–1954), Lieutenant-Bailiff of Jersey, in his preface to a book on Jersey history, wrote in 1935 of the Jerseyman's independence, initiative, application, frugality and integrity, while Henry D. Inglis in his book *The Channel Islands* wrote in 1834 "that . . . love of acquisition, and a strict frugality, form, with independence, another strong trait of Jersey character, is undeniable". Of the Guernseyman he wrote:

It is scarcely to be supposed, that there is any very marked distinction between the characters of the people of Guernsey, and of Jersey. Love of acquisition distinguishes both; and perhaps, in nearly an equal degree; though I confess I have not observed, nor have been able to obtain such glaring proofs of extreme parsimony in Guernsey, as in Jersey. It is certain, however, that they are a thrifty, and a saving people.

Having stated that there were three classes of country people in Guernsey he continued: "All the three classes have however one object:- the accumulation of money; and, generally speaking, all accomplish it." Of the people of Alderney he wrote: "There is one striking difference in the character of the inhabitants of Alderney, and of the other Channel Islands. The parsimony of Jersey and Guernsey, is nowhere to be seen. Indeed, in place of parsimony, improvidence rather, is a characteristic of the people." There is little doubt that the old-time Jerseyman and Guernseyman were pretty tight and, undoubtedly, some still are.

It is certain, however, that Channel Islanders are independent, springing largely from the fact that they live on small islands. An expression frequently used in Jersey until a few years ago was "There's a boat in the morning." It was invariably directed at any non-islander who showed displeasure at something to do with the island. Each island is also very much independent of the others, interests itself in its own affairs and goes its own way. There is also a good deal of inter-insular rivalry, especially between Jersey and Guernsey in the realm of sport.

The islanders are on the whole hard working, enterprising and adaptable and as a result have for many years managed to maintain a high degree of prosperity. It is also true to say that Channel Islanders are hospitable and make good hosts. Their adaptability to changing circumstances is borne out by the way in which, as the centuries have advanced, and old industries have died away, they have developed new ones to take their place, thus keeping their economic sails constantly in the wind.

The Church of England is the established Church of the islands, but many other denominations, notably the Roman Catholics and the Methodists, are strongly represented. Methodists, in fact, predominate in Guernsey.

The nicknames for the inhabitants of Jersey, Guernsey, Alderney and Sark are respectively, 'toad', 'donkey', 'cow' and 'crow'. The parishioners of St. Ouen in Jersey used to be called 'grey bellies', and young ragamuffins from the town of St. Helier in the same island were nicknamed 'town pats'. In Guernsey the parishioners of each parish had a Guernsey-French nickname which may be translated as follows: Castel—'pure-bred donkeys'; Forest—'drones'; St. Andrew's—'the siftings'; St. Martin's— 'ray-fish'; St. Peter's—'beetles'; St. Peter Port—'pasty faces'; St. Sampson's—'frogs'; St. Saviour's—'ants'; Torteval—'donkeys with horse's feet'; Vale—'cockchafers'.

The Channel Islands have produced many people of ability, some of whom have remained at home and risen to the highest offices which the islands have to offer, while others have gone out into the world to seek fame and fortune.

It is noteworthy that a number of Jerseymen have played a part in the history of Guernsey. Among such are two members of the de Carteret family: Geoffroi (died c. 1368), who in 1353 was appointed Prior of the Vale; and Sir Renaud (or Reginald) de Carteret (died 1382), who, with other Jerseymen, re-captured Castle Cornet which the French had taken in 1356. Geoffroi

Wallis or Walsh (died 1471) was appointed Captain of Castle Cornet in 1457. Thomas de St. Martin (died 1515) was appointed joint Governor with Edmund Weston in 1485, but only held the office for a short time. Sir Richard Weston (1469–1542) was Governor for thirty-two years. Helier Gosselin (died 1579) was Bailiff from 1549 to 1562, in which latter year he was deprived of office by Queen Elizabeth I. Samuel de la Place (1580–1637), being unable to reconcile himself to Anglicanism in Jersey, went to live in Guernsey and became Rector of St. Martin's in 1620. Jean de Quetteville (1761–1843) helped to pioneer Methodism in Guernsey. George Le Boutillier (1783–1867) set up business in Guernsey in 1804. He is remembered there for his work in re-founding Elizabeth College, the introduction of gas and the building of Commercial Arcade, St. Peter Port, originally named after him.

Few Guernseymen appear to have played any part in the affairs of Jersey, although some families such as the Fallas and the Fautrats (now extinct) settled there.

These small islands have produced many people famous in their day and generation, and today a number of islanders occupy positions of importance in the world.

Jersey makes a tentative claim to have produced one Arch-bishop of Canterbury, Roger Walden (died 1406), and a Bishop of Peterborough, Francis Jeune (1806–68), who was also Master of Pembroke College, Oxford, and Vice-Chancellor of that university. Before becoming Bishop of Peterborough in 1864, Jeune was Dean of Lincoln and was succeeded in that office by a Guernseyman, Dr. James Amiraux Jeremie (1802–72), Regius Professor of Divinity at Cambridge, who was better known for his lectures, sermons and speeches than for his contributions to ecclesiastical literature. Another Jerseyman, Jean Le Vavasseur dit Durel (1625–83), was Dean of Windsor and is buried in St. George's Chapel. He it was who translated the Prayer Book into French for the use of the Channel Islanders, who in those days were unable, for the most part, to speak English. A Guernseyman, John de Saumarez (died 1697), Dean of Guernsey and Prebendary of Windsor, is also buried in St. George's Chapel.

Jersey has a tenuous claim to having provided one Mayor of London (the title Lord Mayor does not occur until the fifteenth century) in the person of Druge (or Drew) Barantyn (or Barentyn) who held the office 1398-9 and 1408-9 and was five times Member of Parliament for London. Guernsey, undoubtedly, provided two Lord Mayors—Paul Le Mesurier (1793-4) and Peter Perchard (1804-5). Le Mesurier was Member of Parliament for Southwark 1784-96 and Colonel of the Honourable Artillery Company 1794-1805 (Vice-President 1784-93, Major 1793-4). He was also Governor of the Irish Society 1798-1805, Director of the East India Company 1784-1805 and Prime Warden of the Goldsmiths' Company 1802-3. Perchard was President of St. Bartholomew's Hospital 1804-6 and Prime Warden of the Goldsmiths' Company 1786-7. Perchard's daughter, Martha, married Le Mesurier's nephew, John, in 1804.

Many Channel Islanders have served with distinction in the armed forces of the Crown, especially the Royal Navy. The most distinguished naval officer from the islands was that great Guernseyman Admiral Lord de Saumarez (1757-1836), the third son of Matthew Saumarez; he served aboard *Victory*, flagship of the Channel Fleet, for two years, took part in the battle of St. Vincent (1797), was second-in-command at the battle of the Nile (1798) and in 1808 was appointed to the command of a strong fleet in the Baltic; he received the Freedom of the City of London and was an Elder Brother of Trinity House. Lord de Saumarez's uncle, Philip de Saumarez (1710-47), captain in the Royal Navy, omitted the 's' from his surname, originally spelt Sausmarez. He attended a school at Southampton kept by Isaac Watts. There is a monument by Sir Henry Cheere to de Saumarez's memory in the north aisle of the choir of Westminster Abbey; it recounts in some detail the principal events of his career. General Sir Thomas de Saumarez (1760-1845) was Lord de Saumarez's younger brother. Yet another brother, Richard (1764-1835), was a surgeon and writer on medical education. Another distinguished naval officer from Guernsey was Admiral Thomas Le Marchant Gosselin (1765-1857); he was present at several engagements off North America and the West Indies and in 1808 with Sir Harry Burrard, a Jerseyman, aboard, he convoyed a large force of troops to the Tagus and covered the embarkation of the army at Corunna in 1809.

Of Jersey parentage, but born in Guernsey, was Vice-Admiral Sir Charles Le Hardy (1680-1744), whose son was Admiral Sir Charles Le Hardy, junior (c. 1714-80). Le Hardy, junior, was appointed Governor of New York in 1755 and was elected in 1764 Member of Parliament for Rochester, a constituency which he represented for four years. He was Member of Parliament for Plymouth from 1771 to 1780. Then there was Rear-Admiral Sir Thomas Le Hardy (1666–1732), who, like his namesake Charles Le Hardy, junior, became a Member of Parliament, this time for Weymouth; he was buried in Westminster Abbey, where there is a large monument (1732) to his memory by Sir Henry Cheere —it stands in the nave to the south of the great west door.

From Jersey came Rear-Admiral Philip de Carteret (1733–96), who is remembered for his circumnavigation of the world in the sloop *Swallow*, a voyage which took him from 22nd August 1766 to 20th March 1769. The same island produced H. S. H. Philip d'Auvergne, Duke of Bouillon (1754–1816), whose career reads more like a fairy tale than sober fact: in 1773 he was midshipman on the *Racehorse*, one of the vessels despatched by the Admiralty to find the North Pole, and at a later date he was First Lieutenant of 'the saucy' *Arethusa*. By a strange quirk of fate he was adopted by the reigning Prince of Bouillon, a small principality in the Belgian Ardennes, as his heir; but, although he succeeded the prince on his death, he did not enjoy the position for long as the principality was abolished by the Congress of Vienna in 1816. During the Napoleonic Wars d'Auvergne organized from Gorey Castle a secret service which kept in contact with and financed the royalists in Normandy, who were nicknamed 'the Chouans'. He was buried at St. Margaret's, Westminster, the church next to the abbey. Another Jerseyman who had a successful career in the Royal Navy was Vice-Admiral Philip Durell (1707–66), one of whose principal exploits was to assist in the capture of Quebec from the French in 1759 by blockading the city and thus preventing the arrival of reinforcements and supplies. His first wife was his first cousin, a Guernseywoman, Madeline de Sausmarez. He is buried in St. Paul's Church, Halifax, Nova Scotia.

The islands have also produced a number of distinguished army officers of whom possibly the most famous was that eminent son of Guernsey, Major-General Sir Isaac Brock (1769–1812). He entered the army in 1785 and by 1797 was a Lieutenant-Colonel; he distinguished himself in the campaign in Holland in 1799 and was second-in-command of the land forces at the attack on Copenhagen by Lord Nelson in 1801. He died at Queenston

Heights on 13th October 1812, his troops having defeated the Americans and thus saved Northern Canada. The memory of this famous man is perpetuated in two place-names in Ontario, Canada—the first is Brockville, a town in Leeds County, and the other is the Brock Group of the Thousand Islands nearby. Brockville is a county town and serves the United Counties of Leeds and Grenville. A bust of Brock was presented to the town at about 1905 by the General Brock Chapter of the Daughters of the Empire. High up in the west aisle of the south transept of St. Paul's Cathedral is a relief (1812) to his memory by Sir Richard Westmacott. Another Channel Islander who is perpetuated in the name of a town in the North American Continent is Lady Elizabeth Carteret, wife of Sir George Carteret, after whom Elizabeth (originally called Elizabethtown), New Jersey, is almost certainly called. Another Guernseyman who distinguished himself in the army was Major-General George Jackson Carey (1822–1872). He served in the Kaffir Wars 1846–7 and 1850–2 and in the Maori War, August 1863 to August 1865, in which latter he commanded at the siege and capture of Orakau. On 27th May 1865 he accepted the surrender of William Thompson, the Maori chief, and his submission to Queen Victoria. Yet another was Lieutenant-Colonel Thomas Fiott de Havilland (1775–1866). At Madras in India he built the Cathedral and St. Andrew's Presbyterian Church, constructed the Mount Road and built the bulwark or sea wall. After his retirement he devoted himself to the affairs of his native island.

The name de Havilland is derived from the fiefs of Haverland, near Valogne in Normandy. The family settled in Guernsey as early as 1176. Thomas de Havilland fought at the siege of Gorey Castle, Jersey, in 1467 and was rewarded by a grant of commercial privileges, as the result of which he established his son James at Poole, Dorset, and James became mayor of the town in 1494. Captain Sir Geoffrey de Havilland was of this family as are the film actresses, Olivia de Havilland and Joan Fontaine. Another famous military man from Guernsey was Major-General John Gaspard Le Marchant (1766–1812). At school he was considered a dunce, and his youth was full of escapades. However, he joined the army and attracted the notice of King George III, with whom he became a great favourite. He interested himself in the introduction of a better cavalry sword and for his services in this connection two swords were presented to him—one by Lord Cornwallis, Master-General of the Ordnance, and one by a Mr. Osborne of Birmingham, who, as a sword cutler, enjoyed a European reputation. An example of the improved sword was on show in the Lukis and Island Museum, St. Peter Port. Le Marchant became Lieutenant-Governor of the Royal Military College at High Wycombe (later transferred to Sandhurst); he fought in the Peninsula campaign and was killed on 22nd July 1812 at the Battle of Salamanca, where his brigade, supported by Anson's Light Dragoons and Bull's troop of horse, made a famous charge which resulted in a French Infantry division being routed and 1,500 prisoners being taken. A memorial (1812) to Le Marchant by Rossi (designed by J. Smith) is in the north transept of St. Paul's Cathedral. Two Le Mesuriers, uncle and nephew, also had successful army careers. The uncle was Commissary-General Havilland Le Mesurier (1758–1806), who acted as Commissary-General during the winter retreat through Holland and Westphalia to Bremen (1794–5). He entered into partnership with his brother, Paul Le Mesurier, in a merchants' business in the City of London. The nephew was Lieutenant-General John Le Mesurier (1781–1843), the last hereditary Governor of Alderney and eldest son of Governor Peter Le Mesurier, who died in 1803; in 1825 he surrendered the grant of Alderney which had been in the possession of his family since early in the eighteenth century.

Jersey too has produced military men. Of these Major-General James d'Auvergne (1726–99), uncle of Philip d'Auvergne, Duke of Bouillon, had an unspectacular military career. He was equerry to Prince George (later King George III). When he retired from the army he settled in Southampton where he entered municipal life, becoming mayor in 1795. He was buried in All Saints' Church, Southampton, which was destroyed during the Second World War. Lieutenant-General Sir Harry Burrard, Bt., (1755–1813) was born at Vinchelez de Haut Manor, St. Ouen. He entered the army in 1772 and saw service in the American War. He was three times Member of Parliament for Lymington. He took part in the Peninsula War, but was not a success and was recalled. Burrard Street in St. Helier is named after him. Another Jersey military man was Brigadier-General Thomas John Anquetil (1784–1842). In 1804 he was listed among the cadets for the Bengal Infantry. He spent the whole of his military

St. Lawrence's Church, Jersey

career in India and Afghanistan, and was killed during the retreat of British forces from the latter country in 1842. There is a tablet to his memory in St. Helier's Parish Church. Undoubtedly, the most colourful general that Jersey has produced was William Mesny (1842–1919), who became a general in the Chinese Army. He went to sea at an early age, and in 1860, when only 18, deserted his ship at Hong Kong. He learnt to speak Chinese and three years later entered the Chinese Customs. When Gordon went to China Mesny served under him in the Chinese Army. Gordon left China in 1865, but Mesny remained in the army and by 1869 was a colonel. Four years later he was a major-general and in 1886 was promoted to lieutenant-general. He died at Hankow.

The Channel Islands have long been associated with North America. Sir Edmund Andros (1637–1713) was Governor of the Province of New York (the name Andros is a corruption of the English name Andrews). Edmund was the second son of a Guernseyman in the household of King Charles I. In 1660 he was gentleman-in-ordinary to the Queen of Bohemia and in 1672 a major in Rupert's Dragoons. He succeeded his father as Bailiff of Guernsey in 1674, in which year he was appointed by James, Duke of York, to the governorship of the Province of New York; he was knighted four years later. Andros was a great antagonist of Philip de Carteret (1639–82), a Jerseyman who was the Governor of East Jersey (of which Sir George Carteret and Lord Berkeley were the proprietors) and whose authority he disputed. Andros had de Carteret arrested and held prisoner in New York before putting him on trial before a special jury who refused to convict him. Following the death of Sir George Carteret, the Duke of York made a grant of East Jersey to Sir George's grandson and heir in which the right to govern was explicitly included. This put an end to the dispute. On the accession of King James II in 1686, Andros was appointed Governor of New England, which included all English North American settlements except Pennsylvania. In July 1692 he was appointed Governor of Virginia, where he founded William and Mary College. He was recalled in 1698 and six years later was appointed Lieutenant-Governor of Guernsey while he was still Bailiff, the duties of the latter office being discharged by a lieutenant-bailiff. He died at Westminster and was buried in St. Anne's, Soho. An emigrant to North

Peirson Memorial in St. Helier's Church, Jersey
Glass angels in the Lady Chapel of St. Matthew's Church, Jersey

America was John Cabot, who settled in Salem, Massachusetts, about 1700, became a general merchant and founded the Cabot family of that continent. He was the son of Francis Cabot and Susanna Gruchy and was baptized in St. Helier's Church on 7th April 1680. His brother, Francis, also emigrated to America, but returned to live in Southampton. Another brother, George, settled in Boston.

Jersey's best-known artist was Sir John Everett Millais, Bt., (1829–96), who became President of the Royal Academy. He was actually born in Southampton, his father being John William Millais, a Jerseyman of an ancient island family, and was taken to Jersey as a young child. He showed an exceptional talent for art at an early age, and his first pictures were accepted at the Royal Academy Exhibition when he was only 17. Millais became the most fashionable painter of his day and produced a vast quantity of paintings, including such famous works as "Christ in the House of His Parents", "Ophelia", "John Ruskin", "My First Sermon", "My Second Sermon", "The Boyhood of Raleigh" and "Bubbles". The last mentioned picture was a portrait of his little grandson, William James, which, much to Millais' horror, was purchased by a famous firm of soap manufacturers from the magazine proprietors who had originally bought it, and used for advertising purposes. The portrait of his daughter, Alice, entitled "The Picture of Health" hangs in the Barreau Art Gallery at the Museum in St. Helier, together with three other examples of his work. Millais was buried in St. Paul's Cathedral, the Royal Academy undertaking the arrangements for the funeral, and numbered among the pallbearers were Holman Hunt and Sir Henry Irving.

The most famous Jerseywoman was undoubtedly Lillie Langtry, the 'Jersey Lily', a beauty, woman of the world and actress. Her name before her first marriage was Emilie Charlotte Le Breton; Lillie was a nickname. She was born on 13th October 1853 at St. Saviour's Rectory (now a private house called La Belle Maison), her father being the Very Reverend William Corbet Le Breton, Dean of Jersey and Rector of St. Saviour. In 1874 she married Edward Langtry, who died in 1897. Her second husband was Hugo de Bathe, whom she married in 1899 and who, in 1907, succeeded to a baronetcy. John Millais painted a portrait of her holding a lily and called it "A Jersey Lily", which was the origin of the sobriquet by which she became widely known. She mixed in high society and her friendship with the Prince of Wales (later King Edward VII) attracted public attention. As an actress (not a very good one), she toured the British Isles, the United States and South Africa. She died at Monte Carlo and was buried in St. Saviour's Churchyard, Jersey, where a marble bust of her on a granite base marks her grave; there is also a tablet to her memory in the church. Both John Millais and Lillie Langtry are depicted among a number of other celebrities in the picture "The Private View at the Royal Academy 1881" by W. P. Frith, R.A., which was exhibited in the Bi-centenary Exhibition of the Royal Academy.

Sir Edward Seymour George Hicks (1871–1949), the actor-manager, was a Jerseyman. He married Mary Ellaline Lewin Terriss (known in the theatre as Ellaline Terriss) in 1893 when they were both in Arthur Chudleigh's Company at the Royal Court Theatre, London. Hicks was considered the most versatile and brilliant comedian of his day. He played many parts including Scrooge in John Baldwin Buckstone's play of that name and Valentine Brown in Barrie's *Quality Street*. In September 1904 came his great Vaudeville success, *The Catch of the Season*, written by him in collaboration with Cosmo Hamilton, which ran until 1906. He built the Hicks Theatre (now called 'The Globe') in Shaftesbury Avenue, London, and opened it on 27th December 1906 with a production of *The Beauty of Bath*, which was also written by himself and Hamilton.

Another Jerseyman famous in the world of the theatre was Lionel Frederick Leonard, later known as Frederick Lonsdale (1881–1954), the playwright and librettist. His best-known plays are probably *The Last of Mrs. Cheyney*, *On Approval* and *Canaries Sometimes Sing*. His light opera *The Maid of the Mountains*, for which he wrote the libretto, ran for 1,352 performances at Daly's Theatre, London. He died suddenly while walking in a London street. A writer in the *Daily Express* once described him as a master of the dramatic form. He was almost certainly the only Jerseyman ever to have been received by a President of the United States—Franklin D. Roosevelt.

In passing, it is interesting to note that Henry Albert Butt, the father of Dame Clara Ellen Butt, the famous contralto, was a Jerseyman, being born at St. Martin in 1848.

Another famous Jerseywoman was the novelist Elinor Glyn (1864–1943). The daughter of Douglas Sutherland, a civil engineer, she married Clayton Glyn, J.P., in 1892. Elinor Glyn was an extremely penetrating observer of the environment in which she lived, and her books, despite their imperfections, were read with avidity. In the Hollywood of 1920, where some of her stories were filmed, she began a new career, that of a script-writer. The well-known *Three Weeks* (1907) was regarded as naughty and as usual in such cases was widely read. *It* (1927), a short novel with an American setting, made the word 'it' synonymous with personal magnetism. Elinor Glyn was a prolific writer and enjoyed great international success. A popular edition of her books, issued in 1917, sold over a million copies.

The Channel Islands have produced at least two men who have each founded a famous business—Thomas de la Rue and Jean Martell.

Thomas de la Rue (1793–1866) was born at Forest, Guernsey. In 1803 he was apprenticed to Joseph Antoine Chevalier, a master printer. In 1811 he completed his apprenticeship and was then engaged by Tom Greenslade as editor of a new newspaper called the *Publiciste*, the first issue of which appeared in September 1812. The two men parted company in December of the same year. With financial help de la Rue started his own newspaper the *Miroir Politique* in 1813, a venture which only lasted for two years. He then settled in England where he set up business as a straw hat manufacturer. In 1830 de la Rue with two partners went into the stationery business and the next year saw the first de la Rue playing card. The manufacture of straw hats was given up by the de la Rue firm in 1835, and thereafter they devoted their attention to the stationery and printing business. In 1838 the firm produced a special gold edition of the *Sun* newspaper to commemorate the coronation of Queen Victoria. In 1855 the firm secured the contract for printing the Great Britain fourpenny carmine postage stamp to be followed four years later by a contract to print three denominations of currency notes for Mauritius. Warren de la Rue (1815–89), Thomas' eldest son, who was born in Guernsey, was an extremely able man and played a noteworthy part in the development of the de la Rue Company.

Jean Martell (1694–1753), founder of La Maison d'Eaux-de-Vie Martell, the famous brandy firm, was born at St. Brelade, Jersey, of an old island family. The design of the ancient family seal depicting three hammers (martels) and a bird is now used as the firm's trademark; it is also to be seen on the Martell window above the nave aisle doorway of St. Brelade's Church. Martell spent seven years in Guernsey in the counting house of Laurence Martin before establishing himself in business in France.

It would be wrong to leave the subject of the island's famous men and women without saying a few words about the old Jersey family of de Carteret, many of whose members have played an important part in the island's long history. In fact it is true to say that de Carterets have held virtually every office of consequence that it is possible to hold within the island. They have also achieved fame and fortune outside Jersey. Queen Elizabeth I granted Sark to Helier de Carteret, King Charles II granted Alderney to Edward and James de Carteret and Clement Le Couteur, who, in turn, transferred their rights to Sir George Carteret. James, Duke of York, made a grant of New Jersey to Sir George and Lord John Berkeley. Of the same family were John Carteret, first Earl Granville, the famous Whig statesman, and Robert, the second earl, who was a ne'er-do-well. Some members of the family are buried in Westminster Abbey, where a few of them have memorials.

For centuries Channel Islanders have emigrated to all parts of the world. Many have gone to live in the United Kingdom, many more to Canada, the United States, Australia and New Zealand. Sometimes the surnames have become so changed that the association with the Channel Islands is not immediately apparent. For instance, William Frederick Cody (1845–1917), the famous American showman, commonly known as Buffalo Bill, was descended from the Jersey family of Le Caudey. Such changes of name resulted from the difficulty found in pronouncing the French-sounding names—for example, the surname 'Langlois' became 'English'.

Nowadays there are better opportunities within the islands for young people than ever before, but even so their scope is limited and many leave to take advantage of the greater opportunities which are available elsewhere.

For both the native islanders and 'the residents' the islands offer as pleasant a life as that in most places and considerably more so than in a great many. The communities on the islands are very

active, both in business and in leisure. There is practically no un-
employment and, with taxation low in comparison with the
United Kingdom and no estate duty, a good standard of living is
generally maintained. There is virtually no party politics, and
little interest is taken in British politics, unless the islands are likely
to be affected. At times there are grumbles about the activities of
the local legislatures, and on occasion some matter which is under
discussion becomes the subject of controversy. The local newspapers, the *Jersey Evening Post* and the *Guernsey Evening Press*,
known familiarly as *The Post* and *The Press*, and the *Alderney
Journal*, a fortnightly, are avidly read in the islands which they
serve.

A great interest is taken in sport, whether in the islands or
outside and most games are played. The highlight of the soccer
season is the Muratti, an insular sporting event which corresponds
to a lesser degree with the F.A. Cup Final at Wembley. The
match takes place alternately at Springfield in Jersey and at the
Cycle Track, commonly called The Track, in Guernsey. In the
latter island the game of softball, a sort of baseball, is played.

Few places in the world of their size can possess so many clubs
and societies as do the Channel Islands, and some, such as the
Royal Channel Islands Yacht Club and the Société Jersiaise, have
very large memberships. Jersey and Guernsey each holds its local
Eisteddfod, which attracts strong support. With air communications connecting the islands so closely with the United Kingdom,
as well as with Ireland and France, not to mention radio and
television, the outside world has been brought much closer, so
making the islanders somewhat less insular than they were.

It is well nigh impossible to say what life in Jersey and the other
islands is like. Each individual has his own idea of his island based
on family, friends, employment and social life. Within each
island (especially Jersey) there are endless social activities. In the
two larger islands there are not only the native inhabitants, but
also many residents who have come to settle—from the United
Kingdom, Ireland, France, Africa and the Far East, the list is endless. Not unnaturally, little groups are formed based upon
common experience, and often one group may be entirely
oblivious of the existence of the others. The islanders are hospitable to all these immigrants—as well they may be, for many of
them are valuable sources of income to the insular exchequers.

Many of these newcomers never quite integrate with the local population and so do not achieve the real feeling of belonging—those who do are after a time indistinguishable from 'the natives'. To know the islands really well it is necessary to be of them, for only then does one truly know all those little things, seemingly unimportant, which are the very things that make them home.

IV

THE CENTURIES UNFOLDED

... these Isles ... have with great commendation
of their constancy persisted faithfull unto the Crowne
of England, and are the onely remaines, that the Kings
of England have of the ancient inheritance of William
the Conquerour, and of the Duchie of Normandie.

William Camden (1551–1623)

The history of the Channel Islands makes a fascinating study. As each written source of information is examined, each older person questioned and memory is explored, so the decades and centuries fall away and the shades of history take substance to a greater or lesser extent according to the information available.

In the beginning the islands formed part of the continent of Europe, but many thousands of years ago they were separated from the continental landmass. They have been inhabited on and off for countless centuries. Evidence of prehistoric occupation abounds in the islands; and there was even more extant in Jersey (and no doubt in the other islands) when Jean Poingdestre (1609–91), a lieutenant-bailiff of Jersey, wrote *Caesarea* (about 1682), a very early work dealing with that island.

The Channel Islands formed part of Gaul, and when that great province, later to become France, was subjugated by the Roman legions, the islands too became part of the Roman Empire. The evidence would seem to indicate that there was no regular Roman occupation, although Roman coins and other traces of the Romans have from time to time been found in the islands. It is said that the Romans knew Jersey as 'Caesarea', Guernsey as 'Sarnia' and Alderney as 'Riduna'. This statement arises from an interpretation placed on the itinerary, which is attributed to the Roman Emperor Marcus Aurelius Antoninus—but whether it is correct or not is a matter for conjecture. As in Britain, Roman power ultimately ebbed away, and for a period the Channel Islands were possibly under Breton influence. Little evidence, however, remains of this period in the islands' history.

The Vikings made their appearance about the ninth century, when they swept down from Scandinavia in their long boats along the northern coasts of Europe. At first they came to ravage and burn and carried off booty to their northern fastnesses; in time, however, they started to settle in various places, one of which was that part of Gaul, now known as Normandy—the land of the Norsemen or Normans. In 911, by the Treaty of St. Clair-sur-Epte, Rollo, the chieftain of this settlement, was recognized as Duke of Normandy by Charles (nicknamed 'the Simple'), King of the West Franks, Rollo in turn acknowledging the King as his suzerain.

The ancient procedure of the Clameur de Haro, which is still invoked from time to time in the islands, is said to have originated as a plea to Rollo for swift and certain justice. The word 'Haro' is supposed to be a corruption of 'O Rollo!' Even today an appeal for help to the mighty Rollo has the effect of an immediate injunction restraining a person from committing an alleged wrong until the appropriate court has been able to give judgment on the matter.

Duke William I, nicknamed 'Longsword', added the Channel Islands to the Duchy about 933. They then became integrated with the mainland part of the Duchy, and whatever form of government, laws and way of life they had previously possessed were largely, if not entirely, swept away. The introduction of the feudal system to the islands dates from this time.

Duke William I was succeeded in turn by Duke Richard I ('the Fearless'), Duke Richard II ('the Good'), Duke Richard III, Duke Robert I ('the Devil' or 'Magnificent') and Duke William II ('the Conqueror'), who became King William I of England. According to Wace (c. 1135–c. 1174), a Jerseyman and a famous Norman poet, Duke Robert I landed in Jersey about the year 1030, as the result of a storm which arose while he was travelling to England with Edward the Atheling, and remained in the island for some time.

The Dukes owned considerable estates in the Channel Islands, as did a number of the religious houses of Normandy. Norman families went to live in the islands, and a number of the old insular families are descended from these original Norman settlers.

To sum up, the Channel Islands were to all intents and purposes a part of continental Normandy, which was in truth the mainland. Rouen was the metropolis for the islands as much as it was for Bayeux and Caen. What is more, the mainland could be seen from all the islands.

Some vestiges of the Channel Islands' Norman origin remain underlying the creeping anglicization which threatens to extinguish their individuality.

On 14th October 1066 Duke William II of Normandy won the Battle of Hastings and became King William I of England, and ever since then the Channel Islands have, with the exception of a few short breaks, been associated with the Crown of England. They are, therefore, with the exception of England, the oldest parts of the British Commonwealth.

On the death of William the Conqueror in 1087, Robert, his eldest son, succeeded him as Duke of Normandy, and his brother, William Rufus, became King William II of England. In 1106, King Henry I of England having defeated Duke Robert II at Tinchebrai, captured the Duchy, and the Channel Islands, as part of it, were again united with the English Crown. In 1135, upon the accession of King Stephen to the English throne, Normandy passed to Geoffrey of Anjou, who ruled in the name of his little son, King Henry I's grandson.

The House of Anjou or Plantaganet provided eight kings of England: Henry II, Richard I, John, Henry III, Edward I, Edward II, Edward III and Richard II. At the accession of Henry II in 1154, Normandy and England were united again and from then until now, with the exception of a few further short breaks, the fortunes of the Channel Islands have been inextricably linked with those of England.

John, Count of Mortain, was appointed Lord of the Islands (probably only Jersey and Guernsey) some time between 1195 and 1198 and succeeded to the English throne in 1199. On 14th January of the following year he granted the Islands of Jersey, Guernsey and Alderney to Piers des Préaux and confirmed the grant five months later.

In 1204 King John lost continental Normandy to King Philip II (Augustus) of France, but retained the Channel Islands. However, before being finally secured by him, it is said that they changed hands more than once. Despite the islanders' loyalty King John took hostages from their leading families, and these he did not allow to return home until 1214.

Some families with possessions both in the islands and in continental Normandy were placed in a difficult position as they had to decide whether to be loyal to King John and forfeit their property on the mainland or to King Philip II of France and forfeit their insular lands. Generally they decided not on a basis of loyalty, but according to their best financial interests, the de Carterets being some of the few to decide on a contrary basis.

There is a strong but unproved tradition that King John granted Jersey its constitutions and that he visited the island.

King John died in 1216 and was succeeded by his son, King Henry III, who in 1226 confirmed that the Channel Islands should continue to enjoy the same liberties as they had done in the reigns of King Henry II and King Richard I. On 2nd May 1230 King Henry III landed in Jersey on his way to St. Malo, which is the first recorded visit to that island by a reigning sovereign.

By the Treaty of Lambeth of 1217, Louis (later King Louis VIII), son of King Philip II of France, ordered the associates of Eustace the Monk to give the Channel Islands back to King Henry III. By the Treaty of Paris of 1259 King Henry renounced all claims to continental Normandy, but there was no specific mention of the Channel Islands. Despite this renunciation, English sovereigns did not entirely forget their claim to Normandy, for as late as the coronation of King George III in 1761 someone representing the Duke of Normandy walked in the Abbey procession and took precedence over the Archbishop of Canterbury.

In 1337 Thomas Ferrers, Warden of the Islands, was ordered to levy and array all men capable of bearing arms and form them into companies of thousands, hundreds and twenties and to have them well armed and ready to defend the islands. Thirty-three years later King Edward III ordered the Channel Islanders to remain in the islands and to be armed according to their means and to hold themselves ready to defend the islands from attack. It has been suggested that these two orders represented stages in the formation of the Channel Islands' Militias. No doubt, long before 1337 the men of the islands were called upon to defend their homes when threatened by an enemy. The militias were made royal by King William IV in 1831. The insular militias of both Jersey and Guernsey survived into the present century and were two of the most ancient fighting forces in the British Commonwealth; it was with very real regret that many islanders saw their final disbandment.

The French invaded the Channel Islands twice in 1338, and on the second occasion, which was in September, they captured Castle Cornet and became masters of Guernsey, Alderney and Sark. King Philip VI of France granted these islands to his son John, who in turn granted them to Robert Bertram, Marshal of France, who in 1339 tried unsuccessfully to capture Gorey Castle in Jersey. In August 1345 Castle Cornet was recaptured in three days of fighting by the English, and Guernsey was liberated; in 1356 the castle was again captured by the French, but they only held it for a few months.

England won the great battle of Crécy in 1346 and in 1356 the battle of Poitiers. The latter led to the Treaty of Calais (otherwise called the Treaty of Brétigny) of 1360, by which the French abandoned all claim to the Channel Islands.

Owen of Wales landed in Jersey and Guernsey in 1372, but, although he laid waste the former island, he was unable to take Castle Cornet and as a result departed. The following year Gorey Castle was beseiged by Bertrand du Guesclin, Constable of France, but although he captured the outer defences he did not succeed in taking the castle, which was eventually relieved by the English. Seven years later the French Admiral Jean de Vienne captured Jersey and was driven out two years later.

Early in the reign of King Henry V, in 1414, the alien priories were suppressed and their property seized by the Crown. As a result of this Jersey lost the priories of St. Clement, St. Mary of Lecq, St. Mary of Bonne Nuit, St. Michael of Noirmont and St. Peter, but the priory of St. Helier escaped suppression and survived until the Reformation. The priories of Lihou and the Vale in Guernsey were likewise seized.

In 1461, the year in which Edward IV ascended the throne, the French captured Jersey (probably in the Lancastrian interest) and remained rulers of the whole island for seven years. Pierre de Brézé, Comte de Maulévrier, Seneschal of Normandy, was appointed Lord of the Islands by King Louis XI of France. The following year he promulgated ordinances confirming the constitution and privileges of the island. The first recorded use of the name 'Mont Orgueil' (Mount Pride) in regard to Gorey Castle occurs in these ordinances. Four years later de Brézé died and was succeeded as Lord of the Islands by his son, Jacques. In 1468 Jersey was recaptured for the Yorkist King Edward IV by the English under Vice-Admiral Sir Richard Harliston. The following year the King granted a charter to the island; in this he acknowledged the assistance given by Jerseymen in the reduction of Gorey Castle, granted to the islanders quittance from tolls in the realm of England and directed that the island should enjoy its liberties and franchises as formerly.

In February 1481 Pope Sixtus IV issued a monition ordering pirates to abstain from attacking Guernsey, Jersey and Alderney under pain of excommunication, etc. This monition was re-issued in March 1483 as a Bull which ordered that the islands and their surrounding waters should be treated as neutral in time of war and that enemy ships and goods be immune from capture within the neutral areas. It was ordered that the Bull be posted on the cathedrals of Canterbury, London, Salisbury, Nantes, St. Pol de Léon, Tréguier and the Church of St. Peter Port. This clearly indicates that at that time St. Peter Port must have been the principal town of the Channel Islands. Although sometimes breached, this privilege of neutrality continued in force until 1689, when it was abolished by an Order in Council.

From early times the Channel Islands were in the Diocese of Coutances in Normandy. M. Le Canu, in his *Histoire des Evêques de Coutances*, lists the Bishops of that Diocese from 525. It would seem that when the Channel Islands became part of the Duchy of Normandy they also became, if they were not already, part of the Diocese of Coutances, within the Province of Rouen. It is thought that an archdeaconary of the Channel Islands may have existed about 1140, but later they were included in that of Bauptois. The Bailiwick of Jersey and that of Guernsey each constitute a separate deanery, and have done so for many centuries. In 1400 the Channel Islands were transferred by a Bull of the Pope at Rome from the Clementine Bishop of Coutances to a Bishop of Nantes, who was unable to occupy his see because it was still in the possession of a Clementine Bishop. In 1496 Pope Alexander VI transferred the Channel Islands from the Diocese of Coutances to that of Salisbury, but this never took effect. In 1499, by a further Bull, Pope Alexander cancelled this transfer and instead transferred the islands to the Diocese of Winchester, again without effect, although the Bull was followed by a letter from King Henry VII to the Bishop of Winchester signifying that the transfer had taken place. Bishop Langton of Winchester exercised jurisdiction in Jersey on 1st January 1500, but from then until 1569 the Bishop of Coutances continued to exercise ecclesiastical authority in that island and he instituted Edward Hamon to the Rectory of St. John as late as May 1557. The Bishop of Coutances might have continued his authority even longer had it not been that he insisted on pressing too strongly for his dues. In passing, it is amusing to note that in 1500 Richard Le Haguais took the precaution of being appointed to the Rectory of St. Brelade both by the Bishop of Coutances and the Bishop of Winchester. The position of the Channel Islands as part of the Diocese of Winchester was once and for all declared in an Order in Council of March 1569, confirming a letter of Queen Elizabeth I of the previous June.

In 1517 Martin Luther, a German priest, nailed his thesis to the door of Wittenberg Castle Church. This was the flame which started a conflagration, which swept through Europe. England and the Channel Islands did not escape the fury of the fire, and by the time it died down the papal authority had been destroyed in King Henry VIII's dominions, the monasteries had been laid in ruins and a Protestant Church established of which he was the Supreme Head. In 1534 there were passed the Annates Act, Submission of Clergy and Restraint of Appeals Act, the Papal Dispensations Act, and two Acts of Succession, all of which applied to "this realm or any other the King's dominions" and to "any person subject or resident within this realm or elsewhere within any of the King's dominions". By an Act of 1547, which was implemented in Jersey by a commission addressed to the Governor, all chantry chapels were closed and their endowments, as well as all obits and endowments for masses and the property of the parochial fraternities, were all seized. In addition, all the church bells, except one for each parish church, were taken and sold, the proceeds being spent on fortifications, after providing pensions for the priests who were dependent on the chantry endowments for their livelihood. Guernsey was more fortunate than Jersey and did not lose her church bells. In 1549 came the first Act of Uniformity, which was followed three years later by the second Act of Uniformity.

The death of King Edward VI in 1553 and the accession to the throne of Queen Mary I brought an abrupt end to the Reformation in the Channel Islands, as in England. Nevertheless, the seeds of the Reformation had fallen on rich soil and the roots of Protestantism had grown deep into the hearts of the islanders, and on the accession of Queen Elizabeth I the islands reverted to Protestantism. However, they favoured not the Church of England but Presbyterianism, and it was not until 1620 that Jersey was made to conform; Guernsey was even more reluctant to do so and did not succumb until 1663.

Sark was inhabited from early times. As early as the sixth century Magloire had established a monastery there in the shelter of the valley running down to the inlet on the north-west side of the island, now called Port du Moulin, and to this day the district in which the monastery once stood is called La Moinerie. Magloire's monastery survived until about 1413. The island together with the other Channel Islands, was part of the Duchy of Normandy. William the Conqueror gave Sark and Alderney to the Abbey of Mont Saint Michel at about 1042. Subsequently, Sark passed into the possession of the Vernon family. William Vernon gave the monastery to the Abbey of St. Mary of Montebourg in Normandy, a gift which was confirmed by his son Richard in 1196. For nearly 300 years Sark was at the mercy of the French, who were constantly raiding it, but during the latter part of the fifteenth century and the first part of the sixteenth century it was left in peace. The island was invaded and captured for King Henry II of France in 1549 and two years later was recaptured for Queen Mary I of England by her allies the Flemings. The story of the recapture is told by Sir Walter Raleigh in his *History of the World*. Sir Hugh Poulett, the Governor of Jersey, caused the three forts erected by the French to be destroyed, but no garrison was installed, and Sark became a haunt of pirates who preyed on shipping as it passed through the islands. Helier de Carteret, Seigneur of St. Ouen in Jersey, obtained permission to colonize Sark in 1563 and in 1565 Queen Elizabeth I granted him the Lordship of the Island on the understanding that he would colonize it with forty men. Sark was principally colonized from

Jersey, although in 1567 de Carteret granted to his friend Nicholas Gosselin, a Guernseyman, the Tenement of Beauregard.

In 1636 King Charles I, at the instance of Archbishop Laud, founded three fellowships, one each at Exeter, Jesus and Pembroke Colleges, Oxford, for natives of Jersey and Guernsey. The first two from Jersey to benefit were Daniel Brevint (1617–95), who became Dean of Lincoln, and Jean Poingdestre, of whom mention has already been made. In 1678 Bishop Morley of Winchester founded five scholarships in Pembroke College, Oxford, for natives of the Islands—three for Jersey and two for Guernsey. The primary object behind the founding of these scholarships was to provide the Channel Islands with clergy of the Church of England. Those to whom these scholarships were awarded were expected to return to the islands after their university education had been completed.

The Channel Islands were involved in the Civil War. Jersey, largely because of the de Carterets and a few other loyal families, declared for the King; Guernsey, on the other hand, declared for Parliament. It is not surprising that Guernsey, strongly Presbyterian as it was, should have been attracted more by the Roundheads than by the Cavaliers. It is possible that if it had not been for the de Carterets and their friends, Jersey, which had also favoured Presbyterianism, might also have been on the side of Parliament.

The years of the Civil War were some of the most colourful in the history of Jersey. Twice the island gave refuge to Charles, Prince of Wales (later King Charles II), and James, Duke of York (later King James II), when they were unable to find refuge elsewhere in the realm. The first occasion was from 17th April to 25th June 1646, and the second from 17th September 1649 to 13th February 1650. In the train of the princes came a retinue of lords and ladies, servants and hangers on. All the characters who then trod the island's stage, including the energetic Sir George Carteret, feature in the diary of Jean Chevalier (1589–1675), a Jerseyman who throughout this eventful period carefully recorded the day to day events which came under his notice. As he was of an inquisitive turn of mind, not much escaped him. This valuable record of those troublous times is preserved in the Museum at St. Helier and has been published by the Société Jersiaise in the original old French in which it was written. It is noteworthy that in 1649, as soon as the news of the execution of King Charles I

St. Ouen's Manor, Jersey
Jersey Christening Bowl, c. 1700

Channel Islands were made in 1779 and 1781. On the former occasion an expedition under the command of the Prince of Nassau attempted a landing at St. Ouen's Bay, but the attack was not pressed home. In January 1781 the French made their last attempt to capture Jersey when an expedition under Philippe Charles Félix Macquart, Baron de Rullecourt, a soldier of fortune, landed at La Rocque by night. Two actions were fought, one at Platte Rocque, where the invaders were opposed by a party from the 83rd Regiment, and one in St. Helier. The Lieutenant-Governor, Major Moses Corbet, was surprised in bed by the invaders at his home, Le Manoir de la Motte, and, believing them masters of the island, signed a capitulation. Major Francis Peirson, the senior officer under Corbet, disobeyed the order to surrender and led the 95th and 78th Regiments, assisted by the Militia, against the French, who were defeated in an encounter at the Market Place in St. Helier. Both Peirson and de Rullecourt were killed; the former was buried in the Parish Church of St. Helier, and the latter in the churchyard.

A curious incident occurred in Guernsey on 24th March 1783, when a mutiny broke out in the 104th Regiment quartered at Fort George. The trouble seems to have been sparked off by the arrival from Portsmouth of some discharged men from the 83rd Regiment. Six days earlier the officers and men demanded that the gates of the fort remain open so as to allow them to go and come at their pleasure. The Lieutenant-Governor gave way to this demand, but by doing so did not pacify the mutineers for long. Early in the evening of the 24th the soldiery started firing on their officers and thus compelled them to withdraw from the fort. Directly what had happened became generally known, the Lieutenant-Governor, supported by the 18th Regiment and the Militia, marched to Fort George, and the mutineers surrendered when they saw the strength weighed against them.

Methodism was introduced into Jersey in 1774, but it took some years to become firmly established in all the islands. Its adherents underwent a period of trial during the early years of the movement from which they emerged triumphant. Methodists were to play a considerable part in the affairs of the islands, and even today they have a strong influence, particularly in Guernsey. Among those associated with the early days of Methodism in the islands are Robert Carr Brackenbury, Jean de Quetteville (of whom mention has already been made) and Adam Clarke. John Wesley gave a great boost to the movement by his visit to the islands in 1787. The matter of Militia drill on Sundays became a sore point with the Methodists, and those who refused to attend met with the displeasure of the authorities in both Bailiwicks. However, they were eventually successful in their opposition and were permitted to drill on week-days instead of Sundays.

The early years of the nineteenth century saw the end of one war with France in 1802 and the beginning of another in 1803. The great victory of Trafalgar in 1805 was followed by the final victory of Waterloo in 1815, and peace descended on Europe. It was to be 125 years before the Channel Islands would again face an enemy across the narrow waters dividing them from France.

After the war was over half-pay navy and army officers came to reside in the islands because it was cheaper to live there than in the United Kingdom. French people also began to settle, especially in Jersey, and a number of them became hotel proprietors. Improved communications made the islands more easily accessible, and as a consequence the first visitors started to make their way there.

On 20th June 1837 Princess Victoria, niece of King William IV, ascended the throne of the United Kingdom of Great Britain and Ireland at the age of 18 years. The visits which she made to the Channel Islands—the first ever by a reigning sovereign to Guernsey—were highlights in the lives of the islanders.

On 24th August 1846 the Queen and Prince Albert made an unexpected visit to Guernsey of only two hours duration, and on the 3rd September of the same year they paid an official visit to Jersey. This was amply recorded in prose, verse and illustration; the most notable of the commemorative publications were those illustrated by J. Le Capelain (1812–48) and P. J. Ouless (1817–85), both local artists of distinction. "Clear, bright and beautiful rose the sun on the morning of the 3rd September 1846," wrote one chronicler in his account of the royal visit. The Royal Yacht, *Victoria and Albert*, stood out in St. Aubin's Bay, and the Queen and Prince Albert were transported to the harbour in the tender, *Fairy*. As Her Majesty placed her foot on Jersey soil at eleven o'clock salutes of guns were fired from Elizabeth Castle and by the Royal Jersey Militia Artillery. A large crowd, including the élite of the island, had congregated at the harbour to greet the

V

LAWS AND LAWMAKERS

> ... yet certainly we may affirme that in the art of
> Government, a little Empire doth nothing differ from
> a greater; whereupon it is, that even these small
> Islands, in imitation of the greater Kingdomes have
> also their "Conventus ordinum", or assembly of the States.
>
> Peter Heylyn (1600–62)

The Channel Islands, which comprise the Bailiwicks of Jersey and Guernsey, together with the Isle of Man occupy a unique position in the British Commonwealth because, although very closely associated with the United Kingdom they are not part of it, neither are they colonies, nor are they as independent as those parts of the Commonwealth which have obtained nationhood, such as Canada. Although by Sections 18(1) and (2) of the Interpretation Act, 1889, the 'British Islands' and the 'British Possessions' are defined as including the Channel Islands, their special status is recognized in the British Nationality Act of 1948. This latter Act provides that "a citizen of the United Kingdom and Colonies may, if on the ground of his connection with the Channel Islands or the Isle of Man he so desires, be known as a citizen of the United Kingdom, Islands and Colonies". The inclusion of this provision in the Act was attributable largely to the efforts of Lord du Parcq (1880–1949), a Jerseyman and a Lord of Appeal in Ordinary, who pressed for it during the Bill's passage through the House of Lords.

As has been mentioned earlier, the Channel Islands were annexed to Normandy around 933, Duke William II became King William I of England in 1066, and King John lost the continental part of the Duchy in 1204. Inaccurate as it is from the legal point of view, 'Duke of Normandy' not being included among the Royal Styles and Titles, some Channel Islanders used to refer (a few of the older generation still do) to the Sovereign as 'Our Duke'. Channel Islanders are proud of their loyalty to the Crown, although during the English Civil War Jersey was Royalist while Guernsey was Parliamentarian. Jersey's loyalty to the Sovereign was elegantly expressed by Philip Falle (1656–1742), a Jerseyman, in 1694 in the dedication of his *Account of Jersey* to King William III, where he wrote:

> Ever since our Ancient Dukes exchang'd their Coronet for that Imperial Crown which Your Majesty now wears, we have been noted for Our Fidelity to our Kings. We Glory not in the Extent or Riches of Our Country which cannot be brought into Parallel with the meanest of those Provinces that constitute Your Great Empire; but we Glory in Our Loyalty, which we have kept unblemish'd to this Day.

King Charles II was grateful for this loyalty which on two occasions enabled him to find refuge in Jersey. Successive Sovereigns have granted charters to the islands conferring, extending and confirming privileges. They have also from time to time conferred on certain local societies the distinction of being designated 'Royal'. The Sovereign is directly acquainted with the affairs of the Channel Islands through the Orders in Council relating to them which come before her. The Sovereign appoints the lieutenant-governors, bailiffs, deans, law officers, the Viscount (Sheriff) of Jersey, receivers-general and rectors of the ancient parishes. From time to time the Sovereign confers honours on persons in the islands. Generally, the awards are made to members of the States of the respective bailiwicks and officials of the insular administrations. The Sovereign is Visitor of Victoria College, Jersey.

The Channel Islands are linked to the Privy Council, both legislatively and judicially. There is a special Committee of Council for the affairs of Jersey and Guernsey. Nowadays, there is no legislation solely by Order in Council. Acts of the Imperial Parliament and Measures of the General Synod are extended to the islands by Order in Council. Acts of the States of Jersey and Projets de Loi of the States of Guernsey receive the Royal Assent by Order in Council. Appeals lie in certain instances from the Court of Appeal of each bailiwick to the Judicial Committee of the Privy Council. It is noteworthy that appeals from the Channel

Islands to the Privy Council were among the first of their kind.

From time to time Royal Commissions have been appointed to investigate various aspects of the constitution, judiciary and laws of the Channel Islands. Records of evidence and reports of these commissions, particularly those of 1847 dealing with the criminal law of Jersey and of 1861 dealing with the civil and ecclesiastical law of that island and that of 1947 dealing with proposed reforms in the islands, are a mine of information for those interested in the local constitutional and legal history.

The office of Home Secretary was created in 1782, since when the holder has been the Minister responsible for matters relating to the Channel Islands. Although in 1801 the Home Secretary was relieved of responsibility for the colonies, he retained it for the islands and the Isle of Man, as it was recognized that they have a special status distinguishing them from the colonies. It is usual for the Home Secretary to make periodic official visits to the islands. He advises the Sovereign on the Crown appointments in the islands, both civil and ecclesiastical, and it is through him that the Royal Prerogative of Mercy is exercised in cases where sentence of death has been passed.

From early times the Sovereign was represented in the islands by an official who bore various titles—Lord of the Islands, Warden of the Islands, or Governor. Jersey has had a governor since 1470 and Guernsey from about the same time. On 3rd November 1494 a Writ of Privy Seal was issued restricting the powers of the Governor of Jersey, and on 17th June of the following year an Order in Council was made dealing with, among other things, the conduct of the governor. Owing to friction between the governor and the bailiff of Jersey, the Privy Council laid down in 1618 that: "The Bailiff shall in the cohue (court) and seat of justice and likewise in the Assembly of the States, take the seat of precedence as formerly, and that in all other places and assemblies the Governor takes place and precedence which is due unto him as Governor, without further question." Generally, the duties of the office were carried out by deputies or lieutenants. Guernsey ceased to have a governor in 1835, Sir William Keppel being the last to hold that office; Jersey ceased to have one on the death of Lord Beresford in 1854. The governors used to be sworn in before the Privy Council.

The duties of the former governors since the offices were abolished have been carried out by lieutenant-governors. The lieutenant-governor and commander-in-chief, as he is designated, of each bailiwick is always a high-ranking service officer and is appointed by the Sovereign by warrant. He is received in audience by the Sovereign before taking up his appointment, which is usually of five years duration. Today, to a large extent, the lieutenant-governor is a figurehead who represents the person of the Sovereign on official occasions. Passports are issued in the name of the respective lieutenant-governors; in appearance they are the same as passports issued in the United Kingdom, except that they bear on their covers either the name Jersey or Guernsey. Under Article 23 of the States of Jersey Law 1966 the lieutenant-governor has the right in certain circumstances to veto a resolution of the States, which confirms the position as it existed before the enactment of that Law. In Jersey the lieutenant-governor, as his title suggests, is a member of the Assembly of Governor, Bailiff and Jurats (a body comparable to a bench of licensing magistrates in England), but rarely, if ever, attends its sittings. Both in Jersey and Guernsey he generally attends the Royal Court on special occasions, such as when an important official is sworn in. He tenders advice to the Home Secretary with regard to appointments to Crown livings. On the Sovereign's official birthday he holds a levée at Government House and during his term of office becomes the patron of a number of local societies. In each bailiwick the lieutenant-governor's salary and establishment are paid for by the States. Under the Jersey and Guernsey (Financial Provisions) Act 1947, the States receive in return from the British Treasury out of the Consolidated Fund or the growing produce of it, a sum equivalent to that received on each island from the hereditary revenues of the Crown. When absent from duty, either on leave or because of illness, the duties of the lieutenant-governor are discharged by a deputy governor in the person of the bailiff of the bailiwick concerned. The lieutenant-governor of Guernsey is represented in Alderney by a service officer resident in the island.

Originally the office of bailiff of each bailiwick was subsidiary to that of the Lord or Warden of the Islands, but with the passage of time it has grown in importance and today the position has been virtually reversed. In each bailiwick the bailiff is both the

chief magistrate and president of the States (the Legislative
Assembly). The Bailiff of Jersey also presides over the Electoral
College and the Bailiff of Guernsey over the States of Election,
which bodies elect the jurats of the respective Islands. Each bailiff
discharges a number of functions almost too numerous to mention. Traditionally, although appointed by the Sovereign, the
bailiff of each bailiwick is the defender and upholder of the
immunities and privileges of his island. In the past there have been
many bitter struggles between the bailiffs and the islanders on the
one hand and the English (later British) governments on the other.
The Bailiff of Jersey is assisted by a qualified and paid deputy
bailiff, who, in his absence, is able to preside over the Royal Court
and the States. He is also assisted by a lieutenant-bailiff selected
by him from among the jurats. The Bailiff of Guernsey is assisted
by a deputy bailiff and a number of lieutenant-bailiffs. Neither
Alderney nor Sark has a bailiff. The civil head of Alderney is the
President of the States Assembly, who is elected and holds office
for a term of three years. He does not preside over the court, as
do the bailiffs of Jersey and Guernsey. The civil head of Sark is
the owner of the lordship of the island for the time being. He is
obliged to attend sittings of the Chief Pleas (the Legislative
Assembly) or, if he is prevented from doing so, to appoint a
representative. The Seneschal, who is nominated by the Seigneur,
is the President of the Chief Pleas.

The bailiffs of Jersey and Guernsey each possess a seal. In 1279
King Edward I despatched to his bailiffs in the Channel Islands a
specially cut seal of office bearing the Royal Arms to be used to
authenticate certain documents. Circa 1290 a separate seal was
sent to each bailiff, but the seal of office originally issued remained
in use at least until 1291. The ancient seal, now in the keeping of
the Bailiff of Jersey, is of great antiquity. It was replaced by a
replica made at the Royal Mint in 1931. On the reverse side of the
seal is a representation either of the arms of the bailiff for the time
being, or, in the case of a bailiff without arms, his initials. The
ancient seal, preserved in the record room of the Guernsey
Greffe, dates from 1472; the present seal was made at the Royal
Mint in 1938. During the French Occupation of Jersey 1461–68,
the Commonwealth and Protectorate 1649–60 and the German
Occupation 1940–45, the seals continued to be affixed to documents. A seal was made for the Court of Alderney in 1745, which

is now lost, possibly as a result of the Occupation, and has been replaced by another. The owner of the Lordship of Sark uses his (or her) seal as the official seal of the island.

Out of gratitude for being given refuge in Jersey during the Civil War in 1663, King Charles II gave to the island a silver gilt mace inscribed with a latin inscription which reads in English:

> Not all doth he deem worthy of such a reward. Charles II, King of Great Britain, France and Ireland, as a proof of his royal affection towards the Isle of Jersey (in which he has been twice received in safety, when he was excluded from the remainder of his dominions) has willed that this Royal Mace should be consecrated to posterity and has ordered that hereafter it shall be carried before the Bailiffs, in perpetual remembrance of their fidelity, not only to his august father Charles I but to His Majesty during the fury of the Civil Wars, when the Island was maintained by the illustrious Philip and George de Carteret, Knights, Bailiffs and Governors of the said Island.

The Royal Mace was carried before the bailiff in the Royal Court and States Assembly even during the German Occupation.

The office of Jurat, which is somewhat similar to that of a justice of the peace, was at one time found in all the islands, and is of great antiquity, dating back to shortly after the separation of the Channel Islands from continental Normandy in 1204. Now the office only exists in Jersey, Guernsey and Alderney, and islanders deem it a great honour to be elected a jurat. Even today the majority of the jurats in both Jersey and Guernsey are natives of their respective islands. In Jersey they are elected to office by the Electoral College and in Guernsey by the States of Election; in Alderney they are appointed by the Home Secretary. In Jersey and Guernsey the jurats sit with the bailiff or other presiding judge when cases are heard before the Royal Court. In each case the bailiff or other presiding judge is the sole judge of law. In Guernsey there is no trial by jury and in what would be expected to be jury cases, the jurats act as a jury. In Alderney the court consists of a chairman and six jurats. The retirement age of a jurat in Jersey is 72 years; the ordinary retirement age in Guernsey is 70 years, but it may be extended to 75 years; in Alderney the retirement age is the same as in Guernsey, but the term of office may be extended by a supplementary commission.

Fliquet Bay on the east coast of Jersey

The law officers in Jersey are the Attorney General, Solicitor General and Autorisé de la Partie Public, and in Guernsey are the Procureur and Comptroller. All or them are appointed by the Crown, except for the Autorisé, who is nominated by the Attorney General for Jersey. Between them the law officers of each bailiwick act on behalf of the Crown and States in all civil, criminal and mixed causes in which they are involved, as well as being the legal advisers to the States.

The judicature of each bailiwick is divided into three parts, the Court of Appeal, Royal Court and Lower Court or Courts. In addition, there is a court in Alderney, and the Seneschal's Court in Sark. In Guernsey a number of the feudal courts survive. The Courts of Appeal date from 1961; the Royal Courts, however, are extremely ancient, dating as they do from the time when the jurats were first appointed, shortly after King John lost continental Normandy. The Royal Court in both Jersey and Guernsey sits in a number of divisions and is competent to deal with all matters except treason.

Each bailiwick possesses an ecclesiastical court of great antiquity, and it has been suggested that the Jersey Court may be even older than the Royal Court. The Ecclesiastical Court of Jersey is made up of the dean, who is president, and his eleven assessors, who are the rectors of the other ancient parishes. Out of the number of the assessors the dean appoints two vice-deans. The court has the following officers: greffier (or clerk), greffier substitut, proctor and advocate. The Guernsey Court is made up of the judge, in the person of the dean, and his nine assessors, who are the rectors of the other ancient parishes; there are also the vice-dean and surrogate, the registrar and surrogate, two proctors, advocates and an apparitor. Both courts deal with ecclesiastical business of various kinds. Unlike the Guernsey Court, Jersey's lost its probate jurisdiction in 1949. Both courts have their official seal: Jersey's is of the pointed ellipse type and bears the arms of the deanery impaling those of the dean for the time being, while Guernsey's is of the more usual circular pattern and dates from 1662.

The Royal Courts of Jersey and Guernsey each has a clerk known as the greffier; the Court of Alderney also has a clerk. Each greffier has his own department, which includes the local land registry. In Jersey the land registry was set up in 1602, when Sir Walter Raleigh was governor; in Guernsey the land registry

The Ecréhous, off the east coast of Jersey
Gorey Castle, Jersey, from the sea with the regatta in progress

was set up about the same time. There is also a land registry in Alderney.

Jersey, Guernsey and Sark each have an executive officer of the court, who is known in Jersey as the viscount (in no way equivalent to the title viscount as understood in the United Kingdom), in Guernsey as the sheriff and in Sark as the prévôt. The viscount is assisted by a deputy viscount and the sheriff by a deputy sheriff and a sergeant. The viscount has a black rod, rather like a large tipstave or bâton, surmounted by a crown, and a small silver oar as symbols of his authority.

The legal profession of each bailiwick is distinct, and lawyers of one bailiwick may not practise in the other. The professions are divided into two groups of practitioners, the advocates and the solicitors. In Guernsey, however, the local solicitors (Le Corps des Ecrivains) were abolished in 1932, although provision was made for those practitioners already admitted to continue in practice. Unlike the system in England, the two branches of the profession are not divided, and advocates and solicitors may form partnerships; advocates not only plead but do solicitors' work as well.

Each island has its own legislature called the States in Jersey, Guernsey and Alderney and as the Chief Pleas in Sark. The States of Jersey consist of the President, Dean, Attorney General, Solicitor General, twelve senators, twelve constables (heads of parishes) and twenty-eight deputies. The States of Deliberation of Guernsey consist of the President, Procureur, Comptroller, twelve conseillers, ten Douzaine representatives, thirty-three people's deputies and two Alderney representatives. The States of Alderney consist of the President and twelve members. The Chief Pleas of Sark consist of the Seigneur, Seneschal, tenants and twelve people's deputies. The States of Jersey and Guernsey each have considerable legislative powers, but the States of Alderney are subject to the Guernsey States of Deliberation in regard to the budget and all matters involving financial expenditure. The States of Guernsey legislate for Alderney on criminal matters; they may also, by ordinance, extend to that island other legislation dealing with certain specified matters. A meeting of the electorate, known as the People's Meeting, is held before each meeting of the States of Alderney so that the convener may inform those present what business is to be discussed at the forthcoming meeting and to give any explanations asked for by the electors. Sark's power to legislate is like that of the States of Guernsey in civil matters and of the States of Alderney in criminal matters. The States of Guernsey have power to legislate for Sark on civil matters, which is rarely used. Each of the legislatures has a clerk, known in Jersey as the States' Greffier, in Guernsey and Sark as the Greffier and in Alderney as the Clerk.

Each legislature governs by means of standing committees, each charged with the direction of a particular aspect of the administration. In both Jersey and Guernsey there is a civil service which implements the policies of the various States' committees. Although the system has its weaknesses, in general it works well.

There are virtually no party politics in the islands, and ordinarily all members of the insular legislatures are independents. Nevertheless, many shades of political opinion are represented among the members. In Jersey this freedom from party politics is a comparatively modern departure and is in happy contrast to the bitter political rivalry of the eighteenth and nineteenth centuries. The Charlots and Magots (see Chapter IV) of the earlier century were succeeded by the Laurel and Rose parties of the latter century. The animosity between the supporters of these rival factions is amusingly described by Henry D. Inglis in *The Channel Islands* (1834) thus:

> It is utterly impossible, for any one unacquainted with Jersey, to form any idea of the length to which party spirit is carried there. It not only taints the fountains of public justice, but enters into the most private relations of life. A laurel, and a rose man, are as distinct, and have as little in common between them, as if they were men, not only of different countries, but of countries hostile to each other. The most admirable proposition, that wisdom and patriotism united, ever contrived, if emanating from one party, would be received with coolness,—or more probably with open hostility by the other. In private society too, the distinction is equally marked: families of different parties, do not mingle; and even tradesmen are in a considerable degree affected in their custom, by these distinctions. I have known laurel rigorously excluded from the chaplets which were among the destined rewards of young ladies at a public musical examination; and one hesitates even, before placing a rose bud in the bosom, or a laurel sprig among a lady's curls.

The law of the Channel Islands is derived from various sources, namely the Common Law (based on the Customary Law of Normandy), Royal Charters, Orders in Council, Acts of the Imperial Parliament, laws emanating from the insular legislatures and confirmed by the Sovereign in Council, as well as regulations, orders and ordinances made either under head legislation or dealing with matters of limited importance.

Jersey and Guernsey each has its own police force, which in the former Island is called the States of Jersey Police Force and in the latter as the Island Police Force. The Jersey force is assisted by a large number of honorary police administered on a parochial basis and consisting (in descending order of seniority) of a constable, centeniers, vingteniers and constable's officers. The constable is the same as the official who represents the parish in the States. In fact, the States' police are subject somewhat to the honorary police, and every case taken to the police court is in charge of a centenier who presents it on behalf of the constable of the parish. In order for this system to be effective it is necessary for the two forces to work in close harmony. The Guernsey force is assisted by a special constabulary. Guernsey is responsible for the policing of Alderney.

Parish administration in the islands varies considerably, although there are some features in common. In Jersey each parish is sub-divided into vingtaines (in the parish of St. Ouen they are called cueillettes) of varying numbers; in Guernsey each into four cantons. In Jersey the head of each parish is the constable, who, as has been said, is also the parish representative in the States and head of the honorary police of the parish. He is assisted in his parochial duties by the honorary police officers already referred to. In addition, each parish has two public trustees. In Guernsey, at the head of each parish are two constables, the senior and junior. There is a parish council called the Douzaine, which, as its name suggests, consists of twelve members. The senior douzenier is called the Dean of the Douzaine. In addition, there are the Procureurs of the Poor. In both islands the civil parish is linked to the ecclesiastical parish, the ecclesiastical side consisting of the rector, churchwardens and almoners (Jersey only). Each parish levies a rate and keeps up its property, including the parish church and rectory. In Sark there is also a parochial administration consisting of a constable, vingtenier and a Douzaine. Both the constable and the vingtenier sit in the Chief Pleas but have no vote. They make arrests as instructed by the prévôt (sheriff) and act as gaolers, a duty rarely required of them on this small island. The constable attends meetings of the Douzaine, but the Seneschal presides. The constable and the vingtenier also collect the rates.

In this rather dull and workaday world it is refreshing to see a little colour and tradition, and it is therefore appropriate at this point to describe the various robes worn by officials in the Channel Islands.

In Jersey the lieutenant-governor wears a red cloak over his service uniform when attending sittings of the Royal Court or States; the bailiff wears a red robe trimmed with black velvet. The first bailiff to wear this dress was that most patriotic of Jerseymen, Jean Hérault (1569–1626). A similar robe is worn by the deputy bailiff, jurats, attorney general, viscount, solicitor general and police court magistrates. The two greffiers and their deputies and the deputy viscount wear black gowns trimmed with black velvet. An advocate, who is an English barrister-at-law, wears the same dress as a barrister, but without the wig; an advocate qualified in France wears the French legal gown, but without the head-dress. The judges of the Court of Appeal wear black gowns. When sitting in the ecclesiastical court, the dean, vice-deans and rectors wear black gowns.

The robes to be worn by the bailiff of Guernsey and certain other officials were prescribed by an ordinance of the Chief Pleas in 1853. The bailiff and the jurats were to wear robes of silk, as then worn by the judges of the superior courts of England, the bailiff's robe to be trimmed with ermine, except where the bailiff should deem it appropriate to wear a black silk robe. In addition, the bailiff and jurats were to wear velvet head-dresses. In fact, the bailiff's present ceremonial robe is not purple, but dark blue. The colour of the silk is not prescribed, but the visible portions of it are of shot silk of a rather beautiful colour somewhere between pink and grey. The jurats' robes are also dark blue with shot-silk linings and trimmings of the same colour as the bailiff's. Unlike in Jersey the jurats wear bands with their robes. The velvet head-dresses worn by the bailiff and jurats are purple. The robes to be worn by the procureur and the advocates were prescribed by an order of the court also in 1853. The procureur and comptroller each wear a black silk gown as worn by a Queen's Counsel in England with a black velvet head-dress. The advocates wear a black stuff gown as worn by English barristers with a head-dress of black cloth. The greffier and deputy greffier each wear a black robe with black velvet head-dress. The sheriff wears a black suit with sword at side and a gold chain. The sergeant wears an usher's robe of black material with a silver chain. The sheriff's sword was purchased in 1853 and is a three-sided one of the rapier type with silver ornamentation on the black patent leather belt and scabbard. On formal occasions, especially in the open air, the sheriff wears a morning suit, top hat, sword, chain and decorations. On similar occasions, the sergeant wears his gown, chain, tricorne hat and decorations. The sheriff's chain has a thin medallion attached to it, which is about two inches in diameter and bears on one side the words "Le Prévôt du Roi de l'Ile de Guernesey" surrounding the Guernsey Arms, and on the other the words "His Majesty's Sheriff of the Island of Guernsey" surrounding the Royal Arms. The chain and medallion date from 1810. The sergeant's chain also has a medallion attached to it, which is slightly larger and much thicker than that attached to the sheriff's; the inscriptions and arms are the same except that the words 'Prévôt' and 'Sheriff' are replaced by the words 'Sergent' and 'Sergeant'. The chain and medallion date from 1860.

In Alderney the chairman of the court wears a very dark blue cloth robe of the style worn by Guernsey's jurats, with facings of shot ruby silk, white bands and a head-dress of very dark blue cloth such as worn by Guernsey's jurats. The dress of the jurats is the same as that of the chairman except that the facings of the robe are of light lilac silk. Female Jurats wear a head-dress similar to that of the male jurats except that it has a slightly smaller and lower crown without the padded pleating above the headband. The clerk of the court wears a plain black stuff robe of the style worn by the greffier of Guernsey with white bands and a head-dress of black cloth of the style worn by the greffier of Guernsey.

Since 1913 the constable of St. Helier has had a chain of office, as have the constables of St. Peter Port since 1932. All the constables of Guernsey possess 'bâtons de Justice' or tipstaves, which are the symbols of their office and have been so since as long ago as 1696. Similar 'bâtons' were generally introduced into Jersey by an Act of the States of 1806 as symbols of office for the constables and centeniers. It is evident from the wording of the Act that the

Constable of St. Helier was already in possession of one. The 'bâtons' vary in size, the large ones are wooden and surmounted by a crown and have painted on the shaft the Royal Arms and cypher and the arms of the island. The smaller ones are similar, but are made of metal and wood and have neither arms nor cypher. The parish trustees of St. Helier have chains of office.

VI

THE TOWN OF ST. HELIER,
ST. AUBIN AND GOREY

> The Town is inhabited chiefly by Merchants,
> Shopkeepers, Artificers, and Retailers of
> Liquors; the Landed Gentlemen generally
> living upon their Estates in the Country.
> Philip Falle (1656–1742)

St. Helier has always been the capital of Jersey. The Town, as it is
familiarly known, stands on the south coast of the island and
occupies a low-lying site surrounded by hills. Looking at the
town from the sea there is to be seen the harbour, flanked on its
western side by Elizabeth Castle and on its eastern side by the
Town Hill, on which stands Fort Regent; in the middle distance,
looking from west to east, are the white bulk of West Park
Pavilion, in South African Dutch style, standing out against the
green slopes of Westmount, the Grand Hotel, and then other
hotels, stores and various buildings which line the Esplanade, with
higher up to the east the main block of Victoria College. Further
in the distance is the mass of the town from which little can be
distinguished except the spires of St. Thomas' and St. Mark's
Churches, and, high up in the background, Almorah Crescent.

St. Helier is within the parish of the same name, does not form
a separate entity and, consequently, is administered just like the
remainder of the parish. It stands on the Fiefs of Mélèches, Prieur
de l'Islet, La Fosse, Payns, Collette des Augrès, Rondiole, Buisson,
Surville, La Houguette, Debennaires, La Motte and Grainville.
With the passing of the years it has expanded and now possesses
a number of suburbs, notably First Tower, Rouge Bouillon,
Georgetown, St. Luke's and Havre des Pas, which in some cases
extend into St. Saviour and St. Clement.

St. Helier is very ancient, although it is difficult to say with any certainty how old it is. One writer states that the first mention of it occurs in the Assize Roll of 1299, but undoubtedly it existed long before, even if only as little more than a village.

For centuries the town remained of small extent. At the end of the seventeenth century it covered a long narrow area bordered by King Street and Queen Street on the north and Broad Street and Hill Street on the south. On the east it extended as far as Snow Hill and on the west to Charing Cross. It should be mentioned that these thoroughfares were not so named at that time. The following century brought about development at the eastern and western extremities of the town. From 1815 development was rapid; new streets were constructed, which doubled, trebled and, possibly, quadrupled the area covered by the town. Many fine crescents and terraces, such as Windsor Crescent (1835), housed those new phenomena of island life 'the residents'.

Just as the town is the capital and hub of Jersey, so the Royal Square is the hub of St. Helier. In fact, the old Market Place, for such it was originally, might be described as the heart of the island. Down the centuries it has been the silent witness of countless events, both great and small. High-sounding proclamations have been read and laws promulgated at "the accustomed place" at the foot of the statue of King George II, which occupies, or is very close to, the site of the ancient market cross; witches were burnt there and malefactors were whipped through it on their way from the court house (on its southern side) to the prison; prisoners were exposed there in the cage awaiting trial, and wrongdoers were pilloried there for their misdeeds. The square has echoed with the sound of fighting and the shouts and threats of rioters; it has been the scene of pomp and circumstance and military ceremonial. Probably the most moving occasion ever to have been witnessed there was when it was filled with a silent crowd listening to Mr. Winston Churchill making his VE-Day speech.

Especially in summer, when the horse-chestnut trees bordering it are in leaf, the square is the most attractive part of the town, with just a touch of a continental atmosphere. When the weather is fine, the numerous benches, which line it on every side, are filled with local people and visitors, and especially with old men with memories watching the world go by.

The square is lined with buildings. Along its southern side from east to west stand the States' Chamber, the Royal Court

House, the public library and the States' Building. Although un-prepossessing from the outside, the States' Chamber has a pleasing interior designed in the Jacobean style. The Royal Court House has occupied its present site since time immemorial. In 1309 the house in which the King's Pleas were held was restored at a cost of twenty sols. Since then the court house has been rebuilt and reconstructed on a number of occasions. The present building dates from 1866. Above the entrances facing the square are the coats of arms of King George VI (bailiff's entrance) and King George II (public entrance); the latter is particularly fine. The court room on the first floor contains an interesting collection of paintings which includes "The Death of Major Peirson" (a copy by W. Holyoake of the original by John Singleton Copley which hangs in the Tate Gallery), Marshal Conway by Thomas Gains-borough, King George III by Philip Jean and Lord Coutanche by Sir James Gunn. The chairs occupied by the Bailiff and the Lieutenant-Governor, said to be Tudor, are worthy of note, as is the finely carved canopy above them incorporating the Royal Arms. Alongside the court house stands the public library. Jersey's original public library was founded in 1736 by Philip Falle (1656–1742), who was for many years rector of Shenley in Hertfordshire, as well as being a canon of Durham Cathedral. The building which housed the original library still exists in Library Place, to which thoroughfare it gave its name; the stone recording its foundation—which once occupied a position over the entrance to the old building—is to be found on the staircase of the present building. The present library has a pleasing interior and contains a portrait of its founder. The States' Building which completes the block was built in 1931 to house the whole of the States' administration, but, as in so many other places, the civil service has expanded so much that it has outgrown this accom-modation.

Facing the States' Building is the parish church, commonly re-ferred to as the Town Church. Alongside it stands an office block incorporating the church hall (1970, by Taylor Leapingwell).

At the western end of the square is an interesting old building. The lower part was originally the corn market, and for many years the upper part was an assembly room where John Wesley preached in 1787. Today the ground floor is occupied by a bank and the upper floors by one of Jersey's leading clubs, the United

Club. The granite arches of the corn market may be seen in the banking hall.

Nearby stands the picquet or guard-house, which dates from the first decade of the nineteenth century. The colonnade was added in 1835. The drainheads on the north and south sides of the building are marked "Geo III" and bear the royal cypher. The attractive sundial on the south wall was erected by the parish; it was renovated in 1965.

The northern side of the square has little to interest the visitor except perhaps the jeweller's shop at the corner of Peirson Place, part of which is depicted in the painting "The Death of Major Peirson", already referred to. It is believed that the first printing press in Jersey was set up on the first floor of the premises.

On the opposite corner is 'The Peirson', a public house named after the gallant major, the building dating from 1745. Facing it on the eastern side of the square is 'The Cosy Corner' (formerly called 'The Cock and Bottle'), one of Jersey's oldest public houses. Next to it are to be found the headquarters of the Jersey Chamber of Commerce, founded on 24th February 1768, and the oldest Chamber of Commerce in the English-speaking world.

The square is paved in granite, and let into the paving towards its western end is the inscription "Vega 1945", commemorating the visits to Jersey during the German Occupation of the Red Cross ship *Vega*, bringing urgent supplies to the islanders.

Not far from the Royal Square in Pier Road is the museum, headquarters of the Société Jersiaise, the local antiquarian society, which was founded in 1873 and has over 2,000 members. The museum is housed in an excellent example of a merchant's house, which was built for Philip Nicolle in 1815 and was presented to the States in 1893 by J. G. Falle, Jurat, father of Lord Portsea (before he was created a baron in 1934 he was at least the second Jerseyman to be Member of Parliament for Portsmouth), for the use of the Société Jersiaise so long as the society should exist. The museum contains only items of Jersey interest, while in the Barreau Art Gallery, named after Arthur Hamptonne Barreau (1879–1922), are hung pictures either by Channel Islands' artists or of local interest. Included in the museum's collection are many exhibits covering almost every aspect of Jersey life from early times to the present day. Beneath the Barreau Art Gallery are reconstructions of an old Jersey kitchen and an old Jersey bed-room. An outstanding possession of the society is a gold torque, which was discovered during excavations in Lewis Street, St. Helier, in 1889. In size it is second only to the Great Torque of Tara and is 4 ft 7½ ins long and weighs 24 oz (Troy). It was restored at the British Museum in 1973. The museum is also the headquarters of The National Trust for Jersey, founded in 1936, the objects of which are similar to those of the English National Trust. The Jersey Trust has over 680 members and owns 50 properties.

To the visitor St. Helier must be a confusing town, with its maze of narrow streets, each with turnings every few yards. There are so many streets that it is impossible to mention more than a few by name. However, they are well surfaced, and many of the pavements are of granite. For a small town the shops are of a high standard and are well-stocked with every conceivable type of merchandise.

One of the principal thoroughfares is Broad Street, which contains the Head Post Office. At its eastern end is a granite obelisk to the memory of Pierre Le Sueur (1811–53), who was Constable of St. Helier from 1839 until his death. King Street and Queen Street, probably named after King George III and his consort, Queen Charlotte, are two of the principal thoroughfares for shopping. The former is now a pedestrian precinct.

St. Helier has a fine range of covered markets. The New Market (1882) in Halkett Place is a splendid example of its type. The roof, which is largely made of glass, is supported by iron pillars at the top of some of which are the arms of the Island in their proper tinctures. The outer walls dividing the market from Halkett Place and Beresford Street are of fine granite with wide openings filled with iron railings. The gates at the Hilgrove Lane and Market Street entrances are from the previous market and date from around 1803. Incorporated in their design are a cornucopia, bunches of grapes, a peacock and the heads of various animals and birds. In the centre of the market is an ornamental pond out of which rises a particularly delightful fountain. Against the eastern wall of the market, facing the pond, is the market superinten-dent's office, until recently named Bureau de l'Administration, a survival from the past when French was widely used throughout the island's administration. The many shops and stalls are occupied principally by butchers, greengrocers, fruiterers and florists. Business in the market is generally brisk, and it presents a colourful and bustling scene throughout the year. The town possesses another market, the Beresford Market—running from Beresford Street to Minden Place—which is devoted to the sale of flowers, fruit, vegetables and fish.

Almost due east from the New Market, in a commanding position above the town, is Victoria College (by J. Hayward), the island's public school for boys. It was built between 1850–52 and is named after Queen Victoria, who, with the Prince Consort, visited the building in 1859. The original building is constructed of grey granite, is in the Victorian Gothic style and comprises the hall and a number of classrooms. The college has been considerably enlarged down the years. The Howard Hall, which was opened by the Prince of Wales (Duke of Windsor) in 1935, contains a splendid full-length portrait of King George V by John St. Helier Lander (1868–1944), a Jersey artist. The World War I Memorial takes the form of a statue in bronze of Sir Galahad by Alfred Turner; the World War II Memorial takes the form of an art room with a dedicatory panel at the entrance. It was opened by the Duke of Gloucester in 1952.

The town hall (1872—by Messrs Le Sueur and Breé) is situated at the corner of York Street and Seale Street and contains a hall, where the parish assemblies and other functions are held, the municipal offices and the police court, which was opened in 1901. The parish, in addition to its ancient records, owns a collection of municipal plate and chains of office, as well as a number of pictures. The principal picture in the collection is "La Repasseuse" (The Ironer) by Jacques Louis David (1748–1825) which hangs in the Constable's Room.

Gloucester Street, named after William Frederick, Duke of Gloucester (who visited the Island in 1817), contains two buildings of interest, namely the general hospital and the opera house (see Chapter XI). The hospital, standing on the western side of the street, originated from a bequest of Marie Bartlett (née Mauger) (1677–1741), whose monument, erected by the States, is to be seen in St. Brelade's Churchyard. The original building was not commenced until 1765; it was severely damaged in 1783 and again in 1859. The present building dates from 1860–63. In the vestibule are two boards on which appears a list of the hospital's benefactors since its foundation. Adjoining the building, on the Parade side, is the chapel built between 1846–48. The foundation stone of the nurses' home, forming the corner of Gloucester Street and Newgate Street, was laid by the Duchess of Kent (Princess Marina) in 1948. A commemorative plaque was unveiled in the new north wing by Princess Margaret in 1959. The prison, appropriately located in Newgate Street, dates from early in the nineteenth century and was visited by Elizabeth Fry in 1833. It is being replaced by a new building at St. Brelade.

The town has a number of parks and open spaces. The oldest of these is the Parade, originally a sandy waste which General Don had levelled in 1811 in order to provide a parade ground. It was later converted into the pleasant gardens which are to be seen today. The statue by P. Robinet in the eastern part of the gardens is of General Don and was erected in 1885. Not far away are the People's Park, the Triangle Park, Westmount Gardens and the Lower Park. A fountain commemorating the bi-centenary of the Jersey Chamber of Commerce in 1968 is to be seen in the People's Park. At the western extremity of the town is First Tower Park, containing archæological remains. On the southern side of the town are Fort Regent, Mount Bingham and La Collette Gardens. The only park on the eastern side of the town, and far and away the most beautiful in Jersey, is the Howard Davis Park which was presented to the island by Thomas Benjamin Frederick Davis (1867–1942) in memory of his son Howard Leopold Davis who was killed in action in World War I. The park was opened and the statue of King George V by Sir William Reid Dick, was unveiled on 30th September 1939.

St. Helier's Harbour, like most harbours, attracts not only those who go there on business, but also locals and visitors alike, who enjoy watching the shipping and the various activities which take place there. The harbour was not always as large as it is today, and for centuries was of the most elementary nature. By 1700 a start had been made in providing a proper harbour, but progress was slow, and it was not finished for many years. In 1720 the States financed the scheme by issuing paper money, and in 1751 King George II gave £200 towards it. Extensions have been carried out as follows: the Victoria Pier 1841–46, the Albert Pier 1846–53 and from La Collette 1973–

At the head of the harbour is the area known as the Weighbridge, so named because the public weighbridge was located there from 1825 to 1970. Close to where the Weighbridge once stood is a statue of Queen Victoria by Georges Wallet, a French sculptor, erected in 1890. It stands 7 feet high on a pedestal of La Moye granite designed by A. Curry, and is carved with the Queen's monogram, the inscription "Érigé par le peuple" (Erected by the people), and the dates 1837 and 1887. At the Weighbridge is the western entrance of the tunnel (1970), carrying the east-west road under Fort Regent.

Bordering the eastern side of the Old Harbour is the thorough-fare known as Commercial Buildings, behind which rises the Town Hill, dominating St. Helier—a very historic part of the town and parish. Until early in the nineteenth century the top of the hill was an open space belonging to the Vingtaine de la Ville. In the seventeenth century the Seigneur of Samarès unsuccessfully laid claim to the hill. In 1785 a prehistoric passage grave was unearthed there, and the stones which formed it were presented by the Vingtaine to Marshal Conway, the Governor, who had it re-erected at Park Place, Wargrave, Berkshire, where it is still to be seen. It would seem that a prehistoric stone circle also existed on the hill, but was destroyed. In 1804 the British government purchased the hill from the Vingtaine for the sum of £11,200 in order to build a fort. The result was Fort Regent, which has dominated the skyline ever since. The signal post, first established early in the eighteenth century, is a familiar sight of the town and still gives notice of shipping movements and weather conditions, while on special occasions it is dressed overall.

Fort Regent is being developed as a leisure centre with an indoor swimming pool, squash courts, militia museum, gardens and other attractions. The parade ground has been roofed in and provides a huge covered area. The Fort is linked to the town centre by a cabin lift from Regent Steps to the eastern bulwarks.

Elizabeth Castle, named after Queen Elizabeth I by Sir Walter Raleigh when Governor of Jersey (1600–03), may be reached on foot from West Park by means of a causeway when the tide is out; there is also a regular ferry service provided by amphibian craft. The area covered by the castle is far greater than would be imagined from seeing it at a distance. The buildings range in age from the sixteenth century to the nineteenth and are in a varying state of preservation. The Governor's House, standing on an elevated height, contains tableaux depicting among others Paul Ivy (*fl.* 1602), the military engineer who designed part of the castle; Wenceslaus Hollar (1607–77), who sketched the building; and Edward Hyde, Earl of Clarendon (1609–74), who wrote much of his *History of the Great Rebellion* while living within its walls. There is also an art gallery and a maritime museum is in the course of being established. Jutting out from the southern side of the castle is a breakwater incorporating a rock to which clings the Hermitage where legend says that St. Helier, the hermit, once lived.

St. Aubin

St. Aubin is a Town of Merchants and Masters of Ships, who first settled in that Place (otherwise not so proper to build on, because too much straitned between Hills and the Sea) for the sake of the adjoining Port, the best and most frequented in the Island.

Philip Falle (1656–1742)

Jersey's second town, St. Aubin, stands at the western end of the bay of the same name, where a pretty valley opens to the sea. To the south-east lie Belcroute Bay and Noirmont Point. In the vicinity are three old and interesting Jersey properties—Noirmont Manor, La Haule Manor and Belle Vue. While a short distance out to sea, on an islet, is St. Aubin's Fort (see Chapter VIII), which may be reached on foot when the tide is out. The town is in the parish of St. Brelade and stands on the Fiefs de Noirmont and de la Reine in the Vingtaines de Noirmont and du Coin. Like the town of St. Helier, St. Aubin has no separate existence from the parish of St. Brelade in which it is situated.

St. Aubin emerges into history in the sixteenth century, and, although from about 1700 to about 1820 it surpassed St. Helier as a port, owing to its superior harbour, it was never the capital of the island. Today it is a small and attractive place with an air of prosperity about it. Its streets diverge from the vicinity of the harbour and where they climb the surrounding hills they do so steeply, with here and there a tortuous bend.

The fort, dating from the sixteenth century, is in quite good repair and is now used for youth activities by the States' Education Department. A pier was built at the fort between 1648 and 1700, attracting many sea captains and merchants to live at St. Aubin. The harbour at the town was built between 1754 and 1819; the

Jersey Battle of Flowers Float—'Disneyland'
The Guernsey lily (Nerine sarniensis)

bollards along the southern arm are from the last St. Aubin's privateer. The first harbour-master was appointed in 1752; later the office was merged with that of St. Helier.

The town consists of six main thoroughfares: Victoria Road (opened in 1844) which is the name given to the coast road from St. Helier as it enters the town, Charing Cross, High Street (La Rue du Croquet), St. Aubin's Hill (Mont les Vaux), opened in 1865, Market Hill (La Rue du Moestre), The Bulwarks (Le Boulevard), and Bulwarks Hill (Le Mont du Boulevard).

The steep High Street is a quaint and attractive thoroughfare lined as it is with a medley of old houses. Peterborough House was the birthplace of Francis Jeune, who became Bishop of Peterborough, hence the name of the house. Le Boulevard, bordering the western side of the harbour, also has its share of old houses, some of which date from the seventeenth century. At its southern extremity stand the headquarters of the Royal Channel Islands Yacht Club, which, according to official records in London, would seem to be the sixth oldest 'Royal' Yacht Club. Its first woman member was Lillie Langtry.

The remains of Le Moulin des Gouttes Pluye (Raindrops Mill) are undoubtedly the oldest pieces of masonry in the town. They are all that remain of the mill, mentioned as long ago as 1269, and were purchased by the parish of St. Brelade in 1926.

A market existed at St. Aubin at least as early as the latter years of the sixteenth century. The premises at present occupied by a bank, although modern, preserve the general form and incorporate the actual granite colonnade and poor box of the market built in 1826, which they have replaced.

The first church built at St. Aubin occupied the now vacant area to the north of the present one in Mont les Vaux. The original building (the foundation stone was laid in 1735) was found to be unsafe, and a new church was opened in 1892. The present Methodist Church on Le Boulevard was opened in 1868 and the Roman Catholic Church of the Sacred Heart in Victoria Road is of much more recent date. All three churches are built of granite.

St. Brelade's Hospital in Mont les Vaux is really a home for elderly people. It was founded in 1757 by Thomas Denton, whose portrait hangs in the building. The funds of the original foundation have been added to over the years.

Moulin Huet with Petit Port in the distance, Guernsey

St. Aubin was linked with St. Helier by railway in 1870, and the line continued in operation until 1936. The station hotel building is all that remains of the railway buildings and installations. Since 1948 it has been the parish hall of St. Brelade. A small garden has been laid out on the site of the station.

Countless visitors have come to the little town, among whom have been a few famous people. Lord Somerset came in 1646; Alfred, Lord Tennyson, the poet, spent a short time on Le Boulevard; Louis Philippe Albert, Comte de Paris, Pretender to the throne of France, resided for a few days at the Somerville Hotel; Lillie Langtry stayed at Noirmont Manor. Victoria Road commemorates a surprise visit made to the town by Queen Victoria in 1859.

Nowadays the greatest annual event in the town's calendar is St. Brelade's Fête, which is held on the Thursday following the Battle of Flowers. On this occasion the approaches to the town are closed to traffic, and the crowd streams in on foot and converges on the main centre of activity by the parish hall. The programme varies to some extent each year, but there is always a carnival procession, containing some of the smaller floats saved from 'The Battle', a beauty competition, and "all the fun of the fair".

There are many attractive views over the town; also from the vicinity of the town across the bay—in the forefront St. Aubin's Fort and then the beautiful curve of the bay; in the distance Elizabeth Castle and, beyond, St. Helier and its harbour; and beyond again, the Town Hill, Fort Regent and the chimney tower of the electricity power station. With the tide either in or out the whole wide prospect makes a splendid sight. At night the entire bay is fringed with lights, the tower of the power station is floodlit and a pink glow in the sky indicates the existence of St. Helier.

Gorey

> Mount Orgueil Castle is a lofty pile,
> Within the Easterne parts of Jersey Isle,
> Seated upon a Rocke, full large & high,
> Close by the Sea-shore, next to Normandie;
> Neere to a Sandy Bay, where boats doe ride
> Within a Peere, safe both from Wind and Tide.
>   William Prynne (1600–69)

Gorey is a district in the east of the island. It stretches from Gorey Village in the west to the extremity of the Castle Green in the east and from the seashore on the south to Gouray Church and Haut de la Garenne on the north. It derives its name from 'Gorroic', one of the three administrative divisions into which Jersey was divided at least as early as 1180. Part of the district stands on the Vingtaine des Marais in the parish of Grouville and part on the Vingtaine de Faldouet in the parish of St. Martin.

Development at Gorey is principally concentrated into two areas—the pier and the village; the former consists of the buildings in the vicinity of the harbour and another group facing the Castle Green; the latter comprises a village street with a few side turnings. The coast road enters Gorey Pier from the west and then turns in a hairpin bend and climbs for a short distance before again turning in a hairpin bend in the direction of St. Catherine's Breakwater. There is a footpath from Gorey Pier to Castle Green which provides a short cut, particularly useful for pedestrians wishing to visit the castle. The land rising steeply behind the Castle Green is known as the King's Warren.

The focal point of the district is Gorey Castle (see Chapter VIII) magnificently situated on a promontory high above the sea. Within its ancient walls are two chapels, St. Mary's and St. George's, each with its crypt. Unfortunately, St. George's Chapel is in ruins. In the keep are a museum in which are preserved various items discovered during excavations carried out at the castle, as well as a series of tableaux depicting the defenders of the castle during the siege of 1373, the Poulett family, King Charles I and Oliver Cromwell, William Prynne and Admiral Philip d'Auvergne. From the top of the keep, looking westwards, there is a splendid view of the fine sweep of the Royal Bay of Grouville, while looking eastwards there is an equally splendid view along the coast to St. Catherine's Breakwater, and beyond to the Ecréhous and Normandy itself. When the visibility is good the spires of Coutances Cathedral may be clearly discerned. On certain evenings during the summer, through the use of floodlights, the castle is converted into a fairy castle which people throng to see.

Gorey was a haven for shipping from early times, but the port as it is today dates from the first quarter of the nineteenth century.

The pier was completed in 1821, the same year in which the States sold the land below the castle for building. When the oyster fishery was flourishing the pier and its immediate vicinity presented a lively scene during the season, but as the fishery declined so did the importance of Gorey. Even then quite large ships used to call at the port, including passenger vessels linking the island with France. After a lapse of some years the shipping link with France was resumed, and it is possible to travel to and fro during the summer months.

Although Gorey Pier is a pleasant place it does not possess, apart from the castle, any old buildings like those at St. Aubin.

The railway from St. Helier to Gorey Village (the station was originally called Gorey) was opened in 1873 and extended to Gorey Pier in 1891; it continued in operation until 1929. The station at the pier, which has been demolished, stood in the vicinity of the present-day bus shelter. The line of the railway track is now occupied by a partly concealed German strong-point and the ornamental gardens which border the seashore.

There are two important annual events in the calendar for this small place, the regatta and the fête, both of which are held during the summer. The regatta has been held for over a hundred years and provides a delightful spectacle on a sunny afternoon, as does the fête, when the pier and its approaches are closed to traffic and for a few short hours are converted into a colourful fairground.

Gorey Village stretches inland from Grouville Common and connects with the road from Gorey Pier to Faldouet. In the village is the Jersey Pottery, which is open to the public and is a great attraction for visitors. Close by the village is Gorey Lodge, which was bought by Sir Tomkyns Hilgrove Turner (1764–1843), Lieutenant-Governor of Jersey 1814–16, and remained in his family for many years. Sir Hilgrove Turner, who was of Jersey descent on his mother's side, is principally remembered for the part he played in securing the Rosetta Stone, now reposing in the British Museum. His name appears on the order of release depicted in the painting called "The Order of Release" by Sir John Everett Millais in the collection of the Tate Gallery.

Situated on an eminence, almost midway between Gorey and Gorey Village, is the church of St. Martin Gouray (commonly called Gouray Church). For some unknown reason, an old form of spelling Gorey was used in the official documentation relating to the establishment of the church.

Mary Ann Evans, known to the world as George Eliot the novelist, stayed in the village at the house now known as Villa Rosa (then called Rosa Cottage) for some weeks during 1857.

VII

THE TOWN OF ST. PETER PORT, ST. SAMPSON AND ST. ANNE

> . . . an haven within an hollow Bay
> bending inward like an halfemoone, able
> to receive tall ships; upon which
> standeth Saint Peters, a little towne
> built with a long and narrow street.
> William Camden (1551–1623)

St. Peter Port, the capital of Guernsey, stands on the east coast of the island, but, unlike St. Helier, the capital of Jersey, it occupies a hilly site. It climbs the hillside from the seafront and the splendid harbour and is intersected by steep and generally narrow streets and even steeper flights of steps. On its southern side are fine cliffs stretching for miles along the coast, and on its northern side is a flattish coastal area. Looking at the town from the sea there is to be seen the harbour, on the southern side of which stands Castle Cornet occupying a similar position in relation to the town as does Elizabeth Castle to St. Helier, and on the front the parish church. Looking from south to north along the skyline may be observed the tower of St. Barnabas' Church, which once housed the Lukis and Island Museum, then the main building of Elizabeth College, the tower of St. James the Less and the Victoria Tower. Looking out to sea from the town on a clear day it is possible to see the islands of Jethou, Herm, Sark, Jersey and Alderney, with the coast of France in the far distance.

St. Peter Port is within the parish of the same name and does not constitute a separate entity and is therefore administered just like the remainder of the parish. The parish of St. Peter Port, which is known as the Town Parish, stands on the Fiefs Le Roi and Rozel and the Franc Fief au Marchant.

The Town, as St. Peter Port is familiarly known, is very

ancient, although it is difficult to say with any certainty how old
it is. In 1350 King Edward III ordered that the town be enclosed
by a wall, but it is doubtful whether the order was ever carried
out; however, some defence works were definitely built, notably
La Tour Beauregard. Six stones, known as Les Barrières de la
Ville (barrier stones) indicate the extent of the medieval town.

For centuries St. Peter Port remained of small extent, but particularly in the late eighteenth century and early nineteenth
century it underwent considerable development. Many new
streets were built containing splendid houses in the Georgian
style, of which Victoria Road and Grange Road are typical. The
districts known as Clifton and Cambridge Park also date from
this period. Today the three main central thoroughfares are the
Esplanade (divided into North Esplanade, Quay, Bus Terminus
and South Esplanade), which, as its name suggests, borders the
harbour, and High Street and the Pollet, which run parallel with
it. There is no focal point of the town like the Royal Square in
Jersey, except possibly the Town Church, alongside which a
Christmas Tree is erected every year. St. Peter Port is smaller
than St. Helier, but what it lacks in size it makes up in quaintness
and interest. It possesses many well-stocked shops, and these look
particularly attractive brightly lit in winter, and especially at
Christmas time when the Pollet, Smith Street and High Street
are decorated with coloured lights.

The Royal Court building is in Rue de Manoir. Alongside it
are St. James' Chambers (1957, by J. R. Couchley), a fine modern
building which houses the law officers of the Crown and the
headquarters of the island police force; behind it is the prison and
in front of it are the offices of a number of advocates. The court
house, a dignified granite structure, was erected in 1799 and
replaced an earlier and very ancient building called 'La Plaiderie',
which was situated just off the Pollet and demolished in 1929.
Alterations were effected to the structure in 1822 to the designs of
John Wilson, and it was enlarged in 1899 on the occasion of the
Diamond Jubilee of Queen Victoria. At the apex of the front
elevation are the arms of the island and the date 1799, and below
and immediately above the main entrance are the Royal Arms.
The building contains the court room, which is used not only for
sittings of the Royal Court but also for sittings of the States, the
Bailiff's Chambers, the Jurats' Rooms, the Law Library, the

office of Her Majesty's Greffier, the Public Registry and, finally, the Police Court. The court room is austere, and the walls are devoid of portraits, except for a full-length one of King George V, a copy by the artist, John St. Helier Lander, of the original portrait which hangs in the Howard Davis Hall at Victoria College, Jersey. Above the Bailiff's chair are the Hanoverian Royal Arms. The Greffe contains a splendid collection of records, including a fine series of charters or letters patent under the Great Seal, the oldest of which dates from 1394. The prison was built between the years 1811 and 1815, replacing Castle Cornet for that purpose.

Going north from the Royal Court House, past the War Memorial, the public garden on the site of St. Paul's Methodist Church and the government office, at the end of Hirzel Street, is Hospital Lane and the Town Hospital, which was founded in 1741 and opened in 1743. The principal buildings, occupying three sides of a courtyard, have a pleasing aspect. The carving of a pelican in her piety above the main entrance is particularly attractive. The block facing the entrance archway bears the date 1824. In the board room is a panel on which appears a list of the benefactors since the hospital's foundation.

Hospital Lane leads into College Street, where are to be found the Church of St. James the Less and across the road Elizabeth College, the island's public school for boys. Named after Queen Elizabeth I, whose arms appear over the main entrance, it was founded in 1563. The main building, which is in the Tudor Gothic style and covered with brown stucco, was designed by John Wilson and dates from 1826-29. The first headmaster was Adrian Saravia (1530–1613), a Fleming, who was one of the team of translators responsible for the Authorized Version of the Bible.

Bordering one side of the college grounds is Upland Road, from which a turning, called Monument Road, leads to the Victoria Tower (1848, by William Collings), built to commemorate the visit of Queen Victoria and Prince Albert to the island in 1846. The tower is 96 feet high and was constructed on the site of an old windmill (Moulin de l'Hyvreuse).

Close by, in Candie Road, stands a fine old house which was given to the island by Osmond de Beauvoir Priaulx in 1899. It is now the premises of the Priaulx Library. This admirable institution is administered by the Priaulx Library Council and is freely available to all persons over 18 years of age.

In the vicinity are two open spaces—Cambridge Park and the Candie Grounds. The former, named after the Duke of Cambridge, became the property of the parish in 1782. An inscribed stone marks the spot where one of the last duels to take place in Guernsey was fought in the late eighteenth century. The latter are pleasant pleasure gardens in which are to be found an auditorium and two statues. One of the statues is of Queen Victoria looking unamused, which is not surprising as the other is of Victor Hugo, who was expelled from Jersey for supporting the writer of a letter, published in the issue of the newspaper *L'Homme* of 10th October 1855, abusing her in no uncertain terms for her state visit to Paris. Hugo's statue is excellent, and on the plinth are these words taken from the dedication of *Travailleurs de la Mer* which he wrote at Hauteville House: *"Au rocher d'hospitalité et de liberté à ce coin de vieille terre normande où vit le noble petit peuple de la mer à l'Ile de Guernesey, sévère et douce."* (On this rock of hospitality and of liberty in this corner of old Norman land where lives the noble little people of the sea in the Island of Guernsey, rugged and gentle). The gardens also contain a number of interesting trees and plants.

From the Candie Grounds it is but a short walk down St. Julien's Avenue to the north end of the Pollet. Towards the top of the avenue, on its southern side, is the South African War Memorial, pleasantly sited in a small ornamental garden. Towards the lower end of the avenue, on its northern side, stands one of the old town pumps.

The Pollet, like the High Street, is narrow and partially cobbled and still possesses a certain old-world air. Near the northern end is the 'Thomas de la Rue', an attractive modern public house. Each room tells a part of the history of that famous Guernseyman and the great business which he founded. On the western side of the street, shortly before reaching Moore's Hotel, is another of the old town pumps. The building of Moore's Hotel is worthy of notice, as is one of the Barrières de la Ville, which is situated almost opposite. In the Pollet are shops selling the traditional Guernsey milkcans and Guernsey sweets ('invented' by Robert Collins).

The High Street is very quaint and attractive. At the Pollet end and on the eastern side should be noted the house where Sir Isaac Brock lived as a child. The ground floor of this once-handsome residence is now occupied by a branch of a multiple store. A plaque records Brock's connection with the property. Down the street on the opposite side should be noted the premises of the Guernsey Savings Bank (founded in 1822), which form the corner of Berthelot Street and have been described rather quaintly as "the only respectable building of an ancient period in the whole length of the main street". From the northernmost end of the High Street may be seen the parish church (commonly referred to as the Town Church) with its spire and the little canopy over the clock bell peeping out at the opposite end, making a fine terminal to a charming thoroughfare. On the High Street side of the church is a commemorative plaque (1969) to Sir Isaac Brock; on the seaward side is another Barrière de la Ville.

There are a number of turnings off the High Street which merit investigation. The first is Smith Street which forms a T-Junction with the High Street; the old name, La Rue des Forges, indicates that at one time several forges were located there. In Smith Street is the post office, alongside which is one of the Barrières de la Ville. Another turning off the western side of the High Street—this time through an archway—is Le Febvre Street, where the Constables' Office occupies a splendid Georgian house, once the property of the Le Marchant family. Slightly further down the High Street on the opposite side under another archway are the Pier Steps leading down to the North Pier. Further along the street on the western side is Commercial Arcade, a pedestrian thoroughfare leading to the markets. In the arcade are to be found two well-known confectionery shops which sell the celebrated Guernsey *gâche* and Guernsey biscuits (see Chapter IX). The sign above the jewellers' and silversmiths' shop at the corner of High Street and the arcade should be noted as it takes the form of a Guernsey milkcan.

Guernsey, like Jersey, has a fine series of markets. The oldest of these are the French Halles, built in 1780. Next door is a building (1876), formerly housing the Queen's Weights. Opposite are the principal vegetable market and the fish and meat markets. The meat market was erected in 1822 and the arcades in 1830. The whole series of markets, and particularly the fish market, are well worth a visit.

Over the French Halles are the old Assembly Rooms—opened in 1782—where John Wesley preached in 1787. They now house the Guille-Allès Library and Museum and are the headquarters of La Société Guernesiaise (formerly the Guernsey Society of Natural Science and Local Research). The library was founded by Thomas Guille in 1856, and, with the help of his friend Frederick Mansell Allès, it was reconstituted, endowed and much enlarged in 1882, since when it has been known as the Guille-Allès Library; the society was founded in 1882.

A little way from the Guille-Allès and on the same side of Market Street is the 'Golden Lion', an ancient looking public house with bow windows and a colourful sign.

Continuing westward, Market Street gives way to Mill Street, which in turn gives way to Mansell Street. These two last-named thoroughfares are narrow and retain a certain degree of charm. Giving off the northern side of Mill Street is Burnt Lane, where is to be found the Roman Catholic Church of Our Lady of the Rosary (see Chapter VIII). Outside the front of the building are two panels which give the history of the church since its consecration in 1829.

At the western end of Mansell Street is Trinity Church (1788-9) and Trinity Square, which, in fact, is approximately triangular. In the centre of the square is a small garden where stands another of the town pumps, dated 1876, and a horse trough. Just off the square is the attractive old public house, 'Les Caves de Bordeaux', which until a few years ago retained its old-time interior.

Two roads lead back from here into the heart of the town— Bordage and Pedvin Street. The former merges at its northern end into Fountain Street, a fine thoroughfare designed by John Wilson which runs the full length of the markets on their southern side. In this street is to be found another of the Barrières de la Ville, as well as a delightful old tinsmiths' shop where Guernsey milkcans are still made; on looking through the window may be seen two great pieces of tree trunk on which the metal is beaten out. Pedvin Street connects with Hauteville, where is to be found Hauteville House, the home of Victor Hugo from 1856-70, when he was in exile in Guernsey. Hugo purchased the property in 1856. Since 1927 it has belonged to the City of Paris and is maintained as it was in the days when it was occupied by Hugo. The interior is remarkable and in every way, is indelibly stamped with the strong personality of its famous owner. The building contains a great deal of wood carving, some of which was executed by Hugo himself. Starting from the billiard room, the visitor is taken on a conducted tour of the house which ends in Hugo's study at the very top, from where may be gained a splendid view of St. Peter Port Harbour and beyond.

Down the hill from Hauteville, in Cornet Street, was the Lukis and Island Museum. It was housed in the former Church of St. Barnabas, which occupies the site of La Tour Beauregard, a fortification probably built in 1357. The collection was derived from an amalgamation of the exhibits of the Lukis Museum and the Candie Museum, with some additional material. Owing to a deterioration in the building the Museum has been closed.

Not far from St. Barnabas' just below the top of Tower Hill Steps is the fifth and last Barrière de la Ville. There was a sixth in Berthelot Street, but it was destroyed.

Opposite the foot of Cornet Street stands St. Peter Port Church and beyond the church are the quay and the harbour. Just around the corner from Cornet Street, nearly opposite the top of the Albert Pier, is the Picquet House (guard-house), built in 1819. At the top of the pier is a bronze statue of the Prince Consort (a copy of the original by Joseph Durham), erected in 1863. Going northwards along the quay, the Victoria Pier and the States' Office are passed. The weighbridge is at the northern end of the North Esplanade, at the landward end of White Rock. Just down the harbour at White Rock let into the harbour wall is a memorial to those members of the civil population who were killed as the result of an enemy air raid on 28th June 1940, and to all other Guernsey civilians who in the island or elsewhere died in consequence of hostilities during World War II. The names of the air-raid victims are listed on the memorial.

To the south of the South Esplanade is La Valette, where there is a sea-water bathing pool and, beyond, an aquarium which has been constructed in a tunnel dating from 1864.

Access to Castle Cornet is gained from the southern arm of the harbour. On the way to the castle the Model Yacht Pond (Victoria Boat Pond), opened in 1887, is passed on the left; a small expanse of water which is the delight of young children. The harbour breakwater continues past the castle until it terminates in a lighthouse at the harbour mouth.

Peter Heylyn wrote in the seventeenth century that "the principall honour and glory of this Island, I mean of Guernzey, is the large capaciousnesse of the harbour, and the flourishing beauty of the Castle".

Castle Cornet, in addition to being an ancient and splendid fortress worthy of the attention of all those who delight in visiting old buildings, contains an excellent series of museums of which the States' Ancient Monuments Committee may well be proud. The collections are devoted to maritime history, paintings of local interest (including many water-colours by Peter de Lièvre), the German occupation, decorations and medals, military equipment and shooting trophies, uniforms, militia uniforms, badges, buttons and insignia of the Channel Islands' militias and an armoury. The militia collections, including silverware, trophies and other relics of the Royal Guernsey Militia, are quite outstanding and are based in part on the Spencer Collection.

St. Peter Port has possessed a harbour from ancient times and was an important port far earlier than was St. Helier. The present harbour was begun in 1580, since when it has been added to from century to century. Today it presents a pleasant sight, particularly in summer when it is filled with pleasure craft and its tranquil waters are frequently disturbed by the ferry boats taking holidaymakers to and from Herm, Jethou, Sark and Fermain Bay.

St. Sampson

> On the north-eastern coast the ugly prosperous
> little town of St. Sampson, lying in the
> middle of stone quarries and greenhouses, can
> boast of a picturesque old church.
>   Edith Carey (1864-1935)

St. Sampson is one of Guernsey's ancient parishes; it stands on the Fiefs of Anneville with its dependencies, des Philippes and Marette, de Henri de Vaugrat, des Bruniaux, de la Fantôme, Le Roi, Franc Fief au Gallicien and Franc Fief de la Rosière. On its eastern side there is an urbanized area, which, although not resembling it, approximates to St. Aubin in Jersey. The town of St. Sampson, lying little more than two miles to the north of St. Peter Port, borders a harbour occupying what was, at one time, the eastern end of La Braye du Valle, a shallow stretch of water dividing the northern extremity of Guernsey, known as Le Clos du Valle, from the rest of the island. The town, like the town of St. Peter Port, is administered with the remainder of the parish.

La Braye du Valle, which covered an area of 300 acres and extended from St. Sampson's Harbour to Grand Havre on the western coast of the island, was drained in 1806 at the expense of the British government. The reclaimed land was sold, and the money realized was spent on road-making. The thoroughfare known as the Bridge, bordering the innermost part of the harbour, marks the spot where there was once a bridge connecting the mainland to Le Clos du Valle. Reference to the bridge is made in an Act of Court as early as 1204.

The town developed from the time of the reclamation of La Braye du Valle and consequently contains no ancient buildings other than the parish church (see Chapter VIII) and two fortifications, Vale Castle and Mont Crevelt, standing respectively on the north and south sides of the harbour entrance.

Vale Castle is of considerable antiquity, has been used as a fortification down the centuries and was in fact used by the Germans during their occupation of the island. On the slope at the approach to the main entrance is a cemetery where Russian troops are buried, some of the 6,000 who wintered in the island 1799–1800. Originally they were buried in a field some distance from Vale Castle, but when the field was sold the bodies were exhumed and reburied where they are today. The fortifications on Mont Crevelt are of more recent date. The martello tower was erected about 1785 and replaced an earlier fort and tower known to have existed as far back as 1680. Like Vale Castle, Mont Crevelt was used by the Germans during the Occupation.

The harbour—the *raison d'être* for the town—was constructed over a number of years from 1820. Originally it was principally concerned with the shipment of granite; nowadays it constitutes a useful relief port for St. Peter Port harbour, especially with regard to the discharge of coal. By the harbour is a clock tower and at the Crocq are two stones of interest. The first, standing 10 feet or more in height, was probably once a menhir or part of a dolmen and now serves as a memorial to Daniel de Lisle Brock, Bailiff (1821–43), under whose presidency the States made the first improvements to the harbour. The second is an obelisk,

27 feet high inscribed with the name of Sir Peter Stafford Carey, Bailiff (1845–83), and the names of members of the States' Committee responsible for the harbour in 1872.

A tramway operated between St. Peter Port and St. Sampson from 1879–1934. The terminus at St. Sampson was in Bridge Road.

To the north of the harbour is the Water Board's desalination plant, while a short distance to the south of the town is Delancey Hill, a public park where tennis and bowls can be played. The granite obelisk erected in 1876 to the memory of Admiral Lord de Saumarez was destroyed during the German Occupation, but, fortunately, the four large bronze plaques which adorned the memorial were saved and are to be seen at Castle Cornet. Also to be seen on the hill are some megalithic remains and a number of fortifications dating from Napoleonic times and the Occupation.

St. Anne, Alderney

The town is situate well neere in the midst of the Isle having a Parish Church and about eighty families, with an harbour called Crabbie some mile off.

William Camden (1551–1623)

St. Anne, the capital of Alderney, is more or less in the centre of the Island. It occupies a flattish site and possesses few landmarks other than the tower of the old Church of St. Anne and that of the new church, which has the same dedication.

The town has a long history, but contains few remains of its past; its present buildings date mostly from the mid-nineteenth century when the island was enjoying prosperity. At the heart of the town is Royal Connaught Square, named after the Duke of Connaught, who visited Alderney in 1905. On its northern side is the former Government House, a dignified granite building set in pleasant grounds, built by John Le Mesurier, the Governor, in 1763, now the Island Hall. The Alderney museum was moved from there to the old school in 1972. The museum contains an interesting collection of exhibits of local interest, including a display made up of items from the Iron Age settlement at Les Huguettes, Longy, which were uncovered while the site of the new golf course was being prepared in 1968. Channel Islands' bank-notes and coins form another display. There is also an arts and crafts section with contributions from local artists, sculptors and potters. Also in evidence is the ship's bell from H.M. Submarine *Alderney*, which was broken up some time ago. Not far from the Island Hall stands Mouriaux House, which was built by Peter Le Mesurier in 1779. In the square are two chestnut trees; the smaller one was planted by Queen Elizabeth II (then Princess Elizabeth) when she visited the island with the Duke of Edinburgh in 1949. The Queen again visited the island in 1957.

Leaving the square on its northern side by way of Church Street, the clock tower and graveyard are passed on the right. The tower (1767), with its spire and a small pyramid at the top of each corner, is all that remains of the old parish church of St. Anne, a primitive building which was enlarged between 1761 and 1767. The church was allowed to fall into decay and was replaced by the present one in 1850. Beneath the clock is a sundial, and over the gateway in front of the tower is a stone with an inscription recording the fact that the public school was built and founded by John Le Mesurier, the Governor, in 1790.

Off Church Street on the right going north is New Street, which, with Victoria Street and Ollivier Street, dates from 1840–1860. On the southern side of New Street stands the court house, with the prison at its rear, the whole dating from 1850. The court room (also used for sittings of the States) on the first floor resembled the Royal Court Room in Guernsey, although it was smaller. It was destroyed by the Germans during the Occupation and rebuilt in 1955 more or less as it had existed previously. On the ground floor are the offices of the Clerk of the Court and the Land Registrar, also the States' Commitee Room where hangs a portrait of Lieutenant-General Sir John Le Mesurier, the last hereditary Governor of Alderney. Over the main entrance of the building are the arms of Alderney. The old prison has been condemned and is never used. A new lock-up has been made out of a spare room in the main building. Under the law prisoners serving more than seven days may be sent to Guernsey.

New Street connects with Victoria Street, which was originally called Rue de Grosnez and was re-named following the Queen's visit in 1854. On the western side of the street going north is the parish church of St. Anne (see Chapter VIII). This fine building was given to the island by the Rev. John Le Mesurier, son of

High Street, showing Town Church, St. Peter Port, Guernsey

1802 Victor Hugo 1885

Lieutenant-General Le Mesurier. The foundation stone was laid in 1847, and the building was consecrated in 1850. The wrought-iron gates and granite arch were erected in memory of the Prince Consort. The parish registers of St. Anne, dating from 1662, are extant.

Victoria Street is the main thoroughfare of the town and contains the principal shops and the Garden of Remembrance to the men of Alderney who died in the two world wars.

At the northern end of the street just by the entrance to Butes Road is the Methodist Church, built in 1852. A short distance away, in Braye Road, is the Roman Catholic Church of SS. Anne and Mary Magdalen, replacing the first Catholic church which was opened in 1848 and destroyed during the German Occupation. The foundation stone was laid in 1953 and the building opened in 1958. The basement of the church is used as a social centre.

Princess Alexandra and her husband, the Hon. Angus Ogilvy, visited the island in 1968. The princess unveiled a plaque at Newtown School to commemorate the visit and also planted a Chinese palm.

The narrow granite-paved streets, lined as they are with small brightly painted houses, give the town a somewhat French appearance.

Victor Hugo's statue in Candie Gardens, Guernsey
St. Peter-in-the-Wood, Guernsey, showing sloping site

VIII

BUILDINGS

> The only enemy these old monuments
> have to fear is the sacrilegious hand
> of man.
>
> Edith Carey (1864–1935)

It is impossible to claim that the Channel Islands are repositories for fine examples either of ecclesiastical or secular buildings. Nevertheless, they contain a number of churches and other buildings worthy of notice.

The islands' only ancient buildings are either ecclesiastical or, in a few cases, military, but even these have been considerably reconstructed and restored down the years. The principal categories of buildings in olden times were churches, chapels, fortifications, manor houses, farmhouses, country houses and cottages, watermills, windmills and town houses and cottages. To these have been added in more recent times many other categories including crescents and terraces, markets and shops, schools, hospitals and municipal buildings.

For over 1,000 years Jersey and Guernsey have been divided respectively into twelve and ten parishes. Owing to the lack of any documentary evidence, it is difficult to assess how ancient these divisions are. The opinion has been expressed that the five central parishes of Jersey—St. Saviour, St. John, St. Mary, St. Peter and St. Lawrence—date back to around 475. Physical evidence would indicate that a church or chapel existed on the site of St. Lawrence's Church, Jersey, as long ago as possibly the beginning of the seventh century. Similar evidence would indicate that a church or chapel existed on the site of the Vale Church, Guernsey, as early as the seventh or eighth century. The presence of these buildings would possibly indicate the existence of parishes at that time. In this context it must also be borne in mind that in nearby Coutances a bishopric had been established at least as early as the sixth century and that in Sark St. Magloire's monastery was established in the same century. Some if not all of the other parish churches in Jersey and Guernsey are probably nearly as ancient as St. Lawrence's and the Vale, although they are undocumented until some centuries later.

The names of some of the ancient churches are of interest. In Jersey there are St. Clement of Pierreville, St. John in the Oaks, St. Martin of Grouville, St. Martin the Old, St. Peter in the Fields, St. Saviour of the Thorn, St. Mary of the Burnt Monastery. The last mentioned name indicates the existence of an ecclesiastical building on or near the site of the present church, but which was destroyed in early times, probably by raiders. In Guernsey there are Holy Trinity in the Forest, St. Andrew of the Sloping Apple Orchard, St. Martin of the Bellouse (exactly what this word means is doubtful), St. Mary of the Castle and St. Peter-in-the-Wood.

In Jersey, at any rate, each parish church originated from a chapel, sometimes one of several standing in a single churchyard. The Fishermen's Chapel in St. Brelade's Churchyard is no doubt typical of the primitive parish churches. As the need arose, each church was enlarged, but it is often difficult, if not impossible, to follow each step in the enlargement of a particular church, although certain enlargements may be dated either from documentary evidence or architectural style. Occasionally an extension is dated, as in the case of the south-east chapel of St. Mary's, Jersey, which has the date 1342 carved in Roman numerals on its eastern gable. In St. Peter Port Church appears the date 1466, which probably indicates when the south transept was built. With a few exceptions, such as St. Peter's Church, Jersey, where the north side of the nave was enlarged in 1886, and St. Mary's in the same island, where the south aisle was added in 1840, most of the parish churches had reached approximately their present dimensions before the Reformation. It should be noted at this point that the ancient building of Torteval Church was demolished and replaced by the present church in 1818, the architect being John Wilson. In passing it should be mentioned that the church was dedicated originally to Our Lady, but at some point of time the dedication was changed to St. Philip. In Alderney the ancient church of St. Anne fell into decay and was replaced by the present one in 1850, the architect being Sir George Gilbert Scott. Only the tower of the old church survives. St. Peter's, Sark, dates from 1821; the chancel was added in 1878.

The parish churches of both Jersey and Guernsey have some family resemblance. St. Brelade's Church and St. Sampson's Church are strikingly similar in appearance, and it is to be wondered whether the fact that they also have Celtic dedications has any significance. A feature all these ancient churches have in common is the stone construction of their roofs, the roof of St. Peter-in-the-Wood and that of the south aisle of St. Sampson's being exceptions. The stripping of the plaster from the interior of St. Brelade's and St. Saviour's, Jersey, took place during restorations in the nineteenth century and early this century. The parish churches do not generally reach any appreciable heights of architectural beauty as do many of the parish churches of England. St. Peter Port is an exception, as is the Hamptonne Chapel at St. Lawrence's which dates from 1524. For the most part these ancient churches are commonplace, but, nevertheless, are not unattractive and present various interesting features. Occasionally an ugly feature is to be found, such as the way in which one or two spires in Jersey have been cemented. The hardness of the local granite obviated against delicate and intricate carving and, consequently, little fine work is to be found. The carving on the font at St. Clement's is a noteworthy exception.

At the time of the Reformation the parish churches must have been similar to other comparable churches of the Catholic world. The richness of the stained-glass, statuary and other embellish ments would have been commensurate with the wealth of the islands.

The Reformation brought great changes to the parish churches. All the stained glass and statuary were smashed, as was almost everything else which related to the old form of worship. The churches were thus converted into plain unadorned buildings, which between then and the restorations of last century and the present century had become filled with pews and galleries; some churches even had galleries for smokers. It should also be remembered that for centuries these churches were used for secular purposes—St. Helier's was last used for a meeting of the civil parish assembly in 1830.

An example of a low-side window occurs in a few Guernsey

St. Peter's and St. Saviour's—each possesses an ancient poor-box
to be found inside the church; the box at Forest is dated 1786.
The present box at St. Peter's is a copy of the old one stolen in
1959. With the exception of St. Martin's, all these boxes are alike,
being constructed out of one piece of timber; that at St. Martin's
takes the form of a small cupboard let into the wall.

Monuments inside the parish churches are numerous in both
Jersey and Guernsey. In the former island there are those to
Maximilian Norreys (died 1591) and Major Francis Peirson
(died 1781)—the latter by John Bacon, R.A. (1740–99)—at St.
Helier's, which are of interest, as are those to Elias de Carteret
(died 1640) and Elizabeth Dumaresq (died 1639), his wife, a joint
cartouche tablet, at St. Peter's, and that to Sir Edward de Carteret
(died 1682), at Trinity. Among outdoor memorials there are to
be found those to John Dumaresq (died 1606) and Esther
Dumaresq, his wife (died 1597), a joint memorial of heraldic
interest, at St. Clement's and to Nicolas de Tréguz (died 1586), at
St. Lawrence's.

In Guernsey interesting monuments are also to be found inside
the parish churches. At St. Peter Port there are those to Admiral
Lord de Saumarez (died 1836), Lady de Saumarez, his widow
(died 1849), William Le Marchant & ors. (1834—date of monument) by Sir Francis Chantry (1781–1842), John Collings (died
1820) & ors., Osmond de Beauvoir (died 1810) & anr., Colonel
Sir George Smith, Kt., A.D.C. to King George III (died 1809) &
ors., the last three by J. Bacon, Jnr., Peter Perchard, Lord Mayor
of London (died 1806), Sir Isaac Brock, K.B. (not dated), Rear-
Admiral Thomas Saumarez Brock (died 1875) & ors., as well as a
number to members of the distinguished family of Carey. There
are memorials to members of the families of Andros, Carey, de
Sausmarez, de Vic, Gosselin and Lefebvre at St. Martin's. At St.
Peter's is one to James Perchard, Gentleman of the Most Honourable Privy Chamber of their Majesties Queen Anne and King
George I, who left £1,000 for the poor fund of the parish. At St.
Sampson's two memorials claim attention: one to Thomas Falla,
lieutenant of the 12th Regiment of Infantry, who died at the siege
of Seringapatam on 6th April 1799 of a wound from a solid
cannon-ball weighing 26 pounds, which became lodged between
the two bones of one of his thighs and remained undetected
until after his death, despite examination of the wound by the

regimental surgeon. A remarkable story, but for all that largely corroborated from contemporary sources; the other to Cecil Lerrier Giffard, an officer of the 11th North Regiment, who was killed at Maidan, Northern India, during the Tirah campaign. Beneath the memorial hangs the deceased's sword. There are also a number of interesting outdoor monuments. On the north wall of St. Peter Port church is a plaque (1969) commemorating Sir Isaac Brock, which was presented by the Government of Ontario, Canada, on the occasion of the two-hundredth anniversary of his birth. The oldest outdoor monument is possibly that to Nicholas Torode (died 1602) in St. Saviour's Churchyard, where is also to be found one to the memory of eleven Irishwomen who died when the cutter *Pitt* was wrecked in Perelle Bay in 1819 on her way from Jersey to Falmouth, and another bearing but two words "Ma Mère". At St. Peter's is a memorial to the Reverend Jean Perchard (died 1653), who was rector of the parish from 1606 until his death.

Two Guernsey churches, St. Martin's and Castel, each has a prehistoric sculpture in its churchyard. At St. Martin's, the figure is known as the 'Grandmother of the Cemetery'. It is a rectangular stone pillar terminating in a carved female head and shoulders, serving as a gatepost between the two gates of the churchyard. The sculpture probably dates from the sixth century. The prehistoric sculpture at Castel is carved far more crudely than 'the Grandmother', and there has been only a very elementary attempt to carve a female head and shoulders. The sculpture probably dates from the second or third century. In the churchyard of St. Saviour's in the same island there is a stone gatepost at the entrance from Les Buttes, upon which are carved two crosses, one at the front and one at the back. It is believed that this stone is a christianized menhir.

There are no ancient brasses extant in the Channel Islands. Evidence that they existed is to be found in the matrices of brasses surviving at St. Peter-in-the-Wood and the Vale, Guernsey.

Jersey's parish churches are rich in plate all of which is post-Reformation, except for part of a chalice at Trinity. The plate at St. Helier's and St. Clement's is displayed in glass-fronted treasuries. In addition to the rich store of silver, some parishes possess pewter vessels, as well as copper collecting pots. The latter are believed to be unique to the island. Guernsey's churches also possess a goodly collection of plate, of which the outstanding item is the ancient chalice (about 1525) belonging to St. Sampson's. The same church also owns an interesting collection of pre-Reformation ornaments, which were found hidden in the tower. St. Saviour's possesses a set of four leather collecting pots dating from 1813; they are still in use and are unique in the Channel Islands.

In some churches in both islands are laid up the colours of the former insular militias.

In the museum at St. Helier is a collection of musical instruments, dating from the late eighteenth century and the early nineteenth century. They came from the old church bands which provided music in the churches before the present-day organs. Similar musical instruments are to be seen in Guernsey at Forest, St. Martin's and St. Saviour's.

The ancient parish registers are in the keeping of the rectors. Those of St. Saviour, Jersey, date from 1540; those of St. Peter Port date from 1565 (marriages), 1566 (burials) and 1630 (baptisms). The registers of St. Saviour's, Guernsey, date from 1528, but are incomplete for the first three years.

In both Jersey and Guernsey only a few ancient chapels survive out of the many which once existed. In the former island are the Fishermen's Chapel in St. Brelade's Churchyard, possessing some frescoes, Notre Dame de la Clarté and the Jerusalem Chapel at La Hougue Bie, Rozel Manor Chapel, the crypt of Samarès Manor Chapel, the two chapels in Gorey Castle (see Chapter VI) and the Oratory of St. Helier (commonly called the Hermitage). On the Ecréhous there are the ruins of St. Mary's Chapel. In Guernsey is the Chapel of St. Apolline or Our Lady of Perelle, dating from the end of the fourteenth century. On Lihou are the ruins of the Chapel of Our Lady of Lihou. A chapel is known to have existed on Herm as early as the twelfth century. The date of the building of the present chapel of St. Tugual is unknown, but it may possibly date, at least in part, from the twelfth century, a date indicated by the simple arch, which might be described as Early English.

All the four principal islands possess churches and chapels of more recent date than those previously mentioned. In both Jersey and Guernsey there are so many that it would not be possible to mention them all.

In Jersey only four of these churches deserve mention: St. Matthew's (1840), Millbrook, St. Lawrence, which was substantially reconstructed as a memorial to the first Baron Trent of Nottingham and re-dedicated in 1934; St. Thomas' (1883–87), Val Plaisant, St. Helier; St. Andrew's, First Tower, St. Helier; and the Sacred Heart, St. Aubin.

St. Matthew's Church is noted for its glass, which is all by René Lalique. The windows and side screens are of moulded glass with a lily design; a glass cross above the altar is supported on each side by glass pillars, all of which can be illuminated; the altar and panels of the communion rail are of glass; the Lady Chapel is divided from the nave by a glass screen and behind the altar in the chapel are four glass angels; the font, which is also of glass, is probably unique. Portland stone, Bath stone, Dorset stone and Hopton Wood stone were used in the building.

In Guernsey among the churches and chapels of more recent date are St. James the Less (1818—by John Wilson), which serves as a chapel for Elizabeth College, St. Joseph's Church (1846–51— by Augustus Welby Pugin, who was later knighted; the 150-foot-high spire, 1899, by Pugin and Pugin); St. Stephen's Church (1864, by George Frederick Bodley) and the delightful church of Our Lady of the Rosary (built 1829, reconstructed 1962), with its ceiling resembling the interior of an upturned boat; and the little chapel of Our Lady of Lourdes (1925), generally referred to as Les Vauxbelets Chapel because of its situation at Les Vauxbelets.

Les Vauxbelets Chapel is one of the best-known sights of Guernsey. This unique building was designed by Brother Déodat (1870–1951), who carried out most of the work of building and decoration, although on his death the chapel was completed by Brother Cephas. The structure is diminutive—inside it only measures 18 feet by 10 feet—and is built of concrete encrusted with a kind of mosaic made up of countless pieces of china, collected over many years. The result is far more pleasing to the eye than could be imagined from any description.

St. Anne's, Alderney, is a splendid Victorian church in the transitional style, with a square tower topped by a low-pitched spire. It is built principally of the local stone, with quoins of Caen stone. The nave has eighteen arches, and three steps lead to the chancel with its variegated black-and-white stone floor.

Jersey, Guernsey and Alderney are full of ancient fortifications;

some are intact and others either wholly or partially in ruins. The history of these castles, forts and towers would fill many volumes, but here it is necessary to be selective.

Apart from prehistoric earthworks, a number of which are to be found on the islands, the Nunnery in Alderney is the oldest fortification in the Channel Islands, it being possibly a Roman fort of the fourth century. The fortification, now a private residence owned by the States of Alderney, stands by the seashore on the western side of Longy Bay. The property consists of a curtain wall, some 17 feet in height, enclosing a rectangular area, and the building which is now used as a dwelling. The history of the Nunnery is obscure. One of the few facts known about it is that it was altered substantially in 1793.

Gorey Castle and Elizabeth Castle in Jersey together equate with Castle Cornet in Guernsey. Both architecturally and historically the three fortifications are extremely interesting.

Until King John lost continental Normandy, the Channel Islands formed part of the Duchy and consequently there was no need for fortifications to protect the islands from attacks from that quarter. However, when continental Normandy fell into the hands of the French it became necessary to build castles to prevent the islands from suffering the same fate.

The precise date of the foundation of Gorey Castle, also known as Mont Orgueil (Mount Pride), is not known, but it is certain to have been built shortly after 1204, although down the centuries it has undergone many changes. The castle was once a formidable fortification and virtually impregnable, but with the coming of cannon into general use its importance waned. It would have been allowed to fall into decay had it not been for Sir Walter Raleigh (governor 1600–03) who had a regard for the old place, and his efforts resulted in its being kept in repair; today, unfortunately, the castle is partly in ruins. It saw service during the Civil War and again during the Napoleonic Wars, when it was the headquarters of Philip d'Auvergne, Duke of Bouillon. The castle is unusual in having, like the Tower of London, two chapels within its walls—St. Mary's, which is intact and was for the use of the governor and his household, and St. George's, which is in ruins and was for the use of the garrison. The Harliston Tower dates from the 1470s and the huge Somerset Tower from the 1540s.

Elizabeth Castle, named after Queen Elizabeth I, was begun in 1590 and occupies the site of the Priory of St. Helier. The original building was designed by Paul Ivy, the Military Engineer. The castle was in continuous use as a fortification from the time when it was first built until early in the twentieth century and was modified and added to as occasion demanded.

The building of Castle Cornet is known to have been commenced as early as 1206. Like Elizabeth Castle, it was in continuous use as a fortification from its inception until the twentieth century and was similarly added to and altered to meet changing requirements. It has been suggested that the original castle was built between approximately 1206 and 1256 and that it was not substantially changed until the sixteenth century, when it underwent alterations between the years 1545 and 1558. The keep was destroyed by lightning in 1672.

St. Aubin's Fort built on an islet off St. Aubin in Jersey, is also a venerable fortification, dating as it does from 1542. It underwent many changes during the three succeeding centuries until eventually assuming its present form. The main feature of the building is the original tower (the upper half is a later addition) around which have grown up outer defence works.

Essex Castle in Alderney, like St. Aubin's Fort, was built in the sixteenth century; work was probably started in 1546 and ceased in 1554. The building was reconstructed in the mid-nineteenth century. During the early years of the twentieth century it was used as a military hospital and has now been converted into flats.

Three other ancient fortifications are worthy of mention—Grosnez Castle and Les Câteaux (otherwise called Le Chastel Sedement) both in Jersey, and Ivy Castle (otherwise called either Château d'Orgueil or Château des Marais) in Guernsey. The ruins of Grosnez Castle in St. Ouen stand on a rocky promontory forming the north-west corner of the island. High cliffs rising from the sea bound the site of the castle on three sides; on the landward side are the remains of a wall (which no doubt originally encompassed the site) with a ditch in front, as well as a fine gateway with a pointed arch and traces of a drawbridge which spanned the ditch. Within the enclosed area once stood a building, traces of which survive. Although called a castle, Grosnez was never one in the true sense of the word. It was not intended for permanent occupation, but merely as a place of temporary refuge in the event of invasion. The castle is known to have existed as early as 1373 and to have been in ruins by 1540. Les Câteaux is the name of an ancient earthwork situated in the parish of Trinity and which consisted of outer defences and a rampart or keep. It has been suggested that this fortification originated and was in use between 1204 and 1452, but there is a possibility, albeit remote, that Les Câteaux is prehistoric and not medieval. The ruins of Ivy Castle cover an area of about four acres on the north-east outskirts of St. Peter Port; they include the remains of the ancient chapel of Our Lady of the Marsh. The castle is mentioned as early as 1244 and was made use of as a fortification by the Germans, who built a concrete structure within its walls during the Occupation. The States of Guernsey Ancient Monuments Committee have plans for the restoration of the castle.

The Channel Islands were always vulnerable from attack from France, and, as England was often in a state of war with that country, their fortifications had to be maintained constantly. In wartime the garrisons were brought up to strength, and sometimes new forts were built. Until World War II no major building of fortifications had been undertaken in the islands since the Napoleonic Wars. Jersey, Guernsey and Alderney have many fortifications dating from that period, including an unbelievable number of martello towers. The towers in Jersey differ slightly in design from those in Guernsey. The ultimate in fortifications achieved at that time were Fort Regent (1806–14) in Jersey, and Fort George (1782–1812) in Guernsey. The former survives almost intact, but the latter has practically vanished and now provides a site for a select estate of houses. The surviving German fortifications are ugly and unloved.

The oldest dwelling to be discovered in the Channel Islands, with the exception of the Nunnery in Alderney and some prehistoric habitation sites, is the early long house excavated at Ruette de la Tour at Cobo, Castel, Guernsey. Approximately one-half of the site lies under the road and is inaccessible. It is estimated that five separate houses were built on the same foundation, the earliest dating from 900–1000. Among finds discovered on the site is a beautiful token or ornament carved in bone, depicting a dragon or a fish; it is Celtic and thought to date from around 900.

In Jersey, Guernsey and Sark are a number of manor houses,

which are generally indistinguishable from many houses. However, a few of them in the three islands are a little finer both in size and decoration than some others. In Jersey the most interesting, both architecturally and historically, is St. Ouen's Manor, seat of the Malet de Carteret family. It has, however, undergone substantial restoration. Two notable portraits hang in the house, one of Sir George and the other of Lady Carteret by Peter Lely. The latter is mentioned by Samuel Pepys in his *Diary* thus: "Here now is hung up a picture of my Lady Carteret, drawn by Lilly, a very fine picture, but yet not so good as I have seen of his doing." The most spectacular manor is Trinity, which resembles a French Château, a result achieved by an imaginative reconstruction carried out from 1910–13 by C. Messervy from designs by Sir Reginald Blomfield, R.A. Other manor houses of interest are: Avranches (present house built 1818), St. Lawrence; Diélament, Trinity; La Hague (rebuilt 1753 and 1871), St. Peter; La Haule (1796), St. Brelade; La Malletière or La Maison des Prés, Grouville; Les Augrès, Trinity; Les Colombiers, St. Mary; Longueville, St. Saviour; Noirmont (present house built 1810), St. Brelade; Rozel (built 1770 and enlarged in 1820), St. Martin; Samarès, with fine gardens and a canal, St. Clement; St. Jean La Hougue Boëte, St. John; and Vinchelez de Haut and Vinchelez de Bas, both in St. Ouen. La Haule Manor and Longueville Manor are now hotels.

In Guernsey the outstanding manor house is Sausmarez Manor, St. Martin's. The house dates from five different periods and, unlike St. Ouen's Manor and Trinity Manor in Jersey, has not been restored or reconstructed. A small part of what was probably the original manor house remains which is many centuries old; the second section dates from the sixteenth century; the third is Queen Anne; the fourth is Regency; the fifth is Victorian. The four principal rooms, namely the wainscot room, the drawing-room (1820), the dining-room and the tapestry room are all most pleasing. The Queen Anne house has a fine staircase giving access to the two rooms to be found on each floor. Sausmarez Manor contains a number of interesting paintings, including portraits of Sir Edmund Andros, Captain Philip Saumarez, by Sir Henry Wollaston, and Vice-Admiral Philip Durell, who brought Philip Saumarez's body home after he had been killed in action. This latter portrait shows the Admiral holding a scroll inscribed "A Plan of Louisburg 1745", for the capture of which Canadian town he was largely responsible. Portraits of four generations of the de Sausmarez family hang above the beautiful sideboard in the dining-room. In the same room is a painting, by the celebrated Jersey marine artist Peter Monamy (*c.* 1670–1749), showing the capture of the French ship of the line, *Mars*, by H.M.S. *Nottingham* commanded by Philip Saumarez. On the other side of the chimney breast is another marine picture, this time by Thomas Whitcombe. Silhouettes of some of Thomas de Sausmarez's twenty-eight children are to be seen on the wall of the staircase in the Queen Anne part of the house. Among the many other treasures to be seen are the wedding coat of King James II, the diary of Sir Edward de Carteret (*c.* 1630–98), Bailiff of Jersey; and the log book of H.M.S. *Centurion* (published 1974) kept by Philip Saumarez when he was the ship's first lieutenant on her famous voyage around the world. The façade of the Queen Anne house, built of grey granite with quoins of red granite, is most pleasing. The house is three-storeyed with a hipped roof and dormers. The roof is surmounted by a gazebo. The front elevation is five windows wide. Raised bands mark the division of the storeys, and the windows are straight headed. The main entrance, giving access to the first floor, is by way of a flight of eight steps and a splendid oak door. In front of the house is a croquet lawn and flower beds, and beyond, bordering the road, are white painted railings and gates. The gate pillars are surmounted by the supporters of the de Sausmarez Arms, a unicorn and a greyhound, each holding a shield; the outer pillars bear the family's arms (a falcon displayed). All the carving was executed by Sir Henry Cheere, a leading sculptor of the eighteenth century. Close by this entrance to the manor grounds stands the court house of the Fief Sausmarez. The court room on the ground floor is older than the upper floor, which was added in the eighteenth century. In the first floor room there is a fireplace surrounded by blue and white Delft tiles representing biblical scenes.

Other interesting manor houses in Guernsey are Les Granges (more correctly called Les Granges de Beauvoir), Les Câches and Les Eperons.

La Seigneurie in Sark is the home of the Seigneur, and it was there that La Dame, Dame Sybil Hathaway, D.B.E., lived until her death in 1974. It is not the original manor house built by

Helier de Carteret in 1565, and only became known as La Seigneurie after Suzanne Le Pelley became La Dame de Sercq by purchasing the Lordship in 1730. Like the first manor house, it was originally built in 1565 and was known as La Perronerie. It was probably rebuilt by Jean Le Gros in 1675, the date appearing over the fireplace in the hall; the sundial on the south-west corner of the house is dated 1685 and bears his initials. The windows on the ground-floor front were enlarged in 1732 with granite brought from Jersey, and in the same year chestnut panelling was installed in some of the bedrooms. In 1854 a new wing was added, as well as the tower, which is rather out of keeping with the rest of the building. Many of the old records of the island are preserved at La Seigneurie.

From early times it was the privilege of a Lord of the Manor to have a *colombier* or dovecot in which to keep pigeons. Later the privilege was extended, and certain leading persons who were not seigneurs were allowed to cut pigeon-holes in the front of their houses. Jersey is rich in *colombiers* and possesses no less than eleven of these attractive buildings, which are to be found at the manors of St. Ouen (modern reconstruction), Rozel (conical roof), Samarès, Trinity (modern reconstruction), La Hague (restored), Longueville (rebuilt 1692 and now the property of The National Trust for Jersey), Le Colombier (1669), Les Colombiers (restored), Diélament (rebuilt 1573), which is the largest, La Haule (square) and Hamptonne or La Patente (square, dated 1674). Hamptonne is not generally regarded as a manor, although it was raised to manorial status by King Charles II in 1649. Guernsey possesses one colombier situated at Torteval which belonged to the Fief au Cannely and the ruins of another on the Island of Lihou. In Sark a pigeon house stands at the back of La Seigneurie.

Jersey, Guernsey and Sark possess a great many attractive old farmhouses, some of which are substantial structures. They are all built of stone to a more or less standard plan. The vast majority of these old houses consist of a ground floor and first floor; the old Guernsey and Sark houses had only a ground floor. In the older two-storeyed houses in Guernsey the front door has two windows on one side and one on the other, and there are four windows on the first floor frontage. In Jersey and in the later Guernsey houses the front door is in the centre and has two windows on either

Guille-Allès Library with the French Halles below

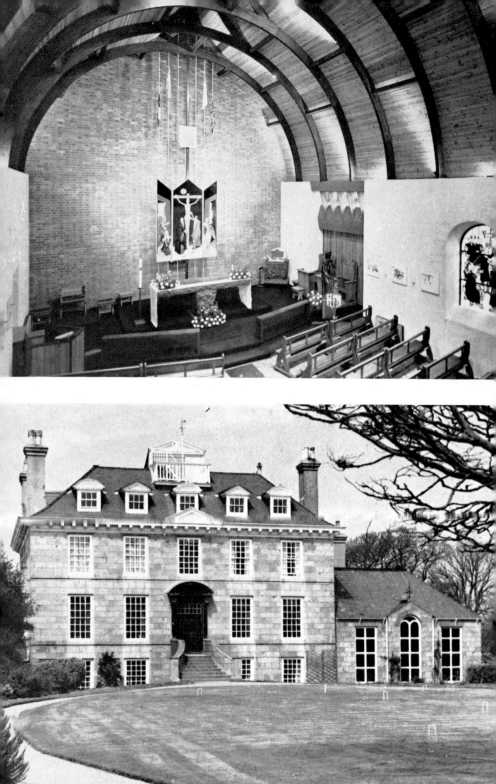

side; there are five windows on the first-floor frontage, one above
each of the ground-floor windows and one above the front door.
The vast majority of the windows are of the sash variety, although
originally the older houses had smaller windows of a different
type. In the older ones the front door opening has a curved lintel
instead of a straight one. In Guernsey, in addition to the stones
forming the arch, there is a second row immediately above them
which is as large as the first. A Jersey and Guernsey custom, almost
certainly not older than the eighteenth century, was for the lintel
of the front door to be carved with the initials of the husband and
wife and the date of their marriage; sometimes intertwined
hearts were also included. There is at least one example of a
marriage stone recording two generations of marriages. Modern
examples of marriage stones are occasionally seen. Originally
these farmhouses were thatched, but nowadays they are all
either tiled or slated. The stones which protrude from the large
chimney-stacks of many of these old dwellings date from when
the roofs were of thatch and were designed to prevent water
seeping underneath it. These stones, as well as the ends of fireplace corbels protruding through a gable wall, are called 'witches'
stones'. It is said that their object was to provide resting places for
witches so as to prevent them from going down the chimney to
rest inside the house. Some houses still possess a circular stone
staircase contained in a tower called a tourelle. Inside the older
farmhouses are found huge fireplaces, either with wooden or
granite lintels.

In the museum at St. Helier are reproductions of a traditional
Jersey kitchen and bedroom, containing many structural features
removed from old farmhouses, as well as original furniture and
household utensils. A similar display may be seen at the Folk
Museum in Saumarez Park, Guernsey.

In a number of Jersey houses and in a few in Guernsey are to be
found niches called bénitiers. No one has been able to say with
any certainty what purpose these served. They have an ecclesiastical appearance, and if they were to be found in churches or
chapels would be designated either piscinas or holy water stoups,
each according to its particular characteristics. Some people say
that they were removed from churches and chapels at the time of
the Reformation; others that similar features may be found in old
houses in Normandy and Brittany and that they are of secular

Interior of Church of Our Lady of the Rosary, St. Peter Port, Guernsey
Sausmarez Manor, Guernsey, showing Queen Anne front

origin and for domestic use. The number of these niches which have survived in private dwellings in Jersey would lead one to believe that some, at least, are of secular origin. In Guernsey there are not so many bénitiers—the finest one is said to be that at Les Grands Moulins at Castel; others occur at Les Effards in the same parish, at La Maison de Haut, St. Peter's, and Les Granges Manor, St. Peter Port.

At the end of some farmhouses is a small dower house representing 'the widow's third', that is a widow's entitlement to the life enjoyment of one-third of her late husband's real estate.

Many of the farmhouses have extensive outbuildings; formerly in Jersey these invariably included pigsties and a presshouse. In the latter were located a circular granite cider trough with a large granite wheel for crushing the apples and a press for extracting the juice from the pulp.

At the entrance of a number of old Jersey farms are two round-headed archways, the larger for vehicles and the smaller for pedestrians.

In addition to the manor and farmhouses there are scattered throughout both Jersey and Guernsey a large number of interesting houses of varying ages. Of these, the most spectacular is undoubtedly La Haye du Puits, Castel, Guernsey, with its attractive turrets. Another fine property in that island is Saumarez Park, an eighteenth-century house belonging to the States and now housing the Hostel of St. John, which is a home for elderly men and women; the spacious grounds, partly laid out as a formal garden, are used for agricultural and horticultural shows.

In years gone by, there were in both Jersey and Guernsey many watermills of which only a limited number remain. The most spectacular in Jersey must have been Le Moulin de Gigoulande, which, with its two mill-wheels, one above the other, stood at the top of St. Peter's Valley, just within the parish of St. Mary; Le Moulin de Haut at King's Mills, Guernsey, also had two wheels, similarly placed.

There were also a number of windmills throughout the islands. Four survive in Jersey—Grouville, Rozel, St. Ouen (possibly early nineteenth century) and St. Peter (1837), but they have all lost their sails. In Guernsey five windmills survive, namely: Le Hêchet or Ozanne's Mill (1825), Ruette Braye, St. Martin's, and Sausmarez Mill in the same parish; Les Vardes, St.

Peter Port, and Mont Saint, St. Saviour's—both cement mills dating from the nineteenth century; and Vale Mill. Sark possesses two windmills, one on Great Sark built by Helier de Carteret in 1571 and the other on Little Sark which was built later.

No really ancient houses and cottages survive in St. Helier or St. Aubin, although the latter does possess some examples of town houses of the seventeenth century. St. Peter Port contains a few really old and attractive houses. Thatch was used extensively for roofing throughout St. Helier until the seventeenth century, but from then on it disappeared rapidly. In Guernsey an ordinance was made on 1st October 1683, whereby all thatched houses in St. Peter Port were to be covered with slates in order to reduce the risk of fire; anyone who failed to comply was to be fined. In St. Helier a number of eighteenth-century houses have been demolished since the end of World War II and scarcely any good examples remain; St. Peter Port is far richer in houses of that period. Both towns were greatly enlarged during the nineteenth century and possess numerous examples of late Georgian, Regency and Victorian houses. St. Peter Port's expansion seems to have begun somewhat earlier than that of St. Helier, and consequently the former has more examples of late Georgian and Regency architecture than has the latter. In St. Helier, Almorah Crescent, Royal Crescent, Victoria Crescent and Windsor Crescent, as well as Clarence Road, Clarendon Road, David Place, Grosvenor Street, Midvale Road, the lower part of Queen's Road, Ralegh Avenue, most of Rouge Bouillon, St. Mark's Road, Stopford Road, Val Plaisant, and many other thoroughfares, were built during the nineteenth century. Much of this development was pleasing to the eye, Almorah Crescent, Royal Crescent and Windsor Crescent being particularly so. Originally, a theatre stood at the centre of Royal Crescent, but it was burnt down in 1863. In St. Peter Port some of the nineteenth-century development is to be seen in Cambridge Park, Doyle Terrace, Eaton Place, Grange Road, Hauteville, Lisle Terrace, Pedvin Street, Queen's Road, Sausmarez Street and Victoria Road.

A nineteenth-century building worthy of notice in Jersey is Corbière Lighthouse, an early example of a concrete structure; it was designed by Sir John Coode and completed in November 1873, the light being lit experimentally for the first time on 24th April of the following year.

A great deal of building has taken place on the islands during the twentieth century, especially in Jersey and Guernsey. Traditional designs have for the most part been abandoned and current fashion as obtaining in the United Kingdom has been followed. The local granite has been out of favour as a building material, although in recent years there has been a partial return to its use, no doubt because of improved machinery for cutting what is a very hard substance. Between the two world wars a great deal of ribbon development took place in Jersey. Both there and in Guernsey the authorities are now very planning-conscious and stringent building controls are in force. These official efforts to preserve the countryside are augmented by those of The National Trust for Jersey and The National Trust of Guernsey, which bodies own a number of properties.

SMALLER THINGS

Coins and Bank-Notes

Many types of currency have circulated in the Channel Islands, but it was not until the nineteenth century that Jersey and Guernsey each had their own copper coinage. No fewer than eleven hordes of Amorican coins were found in Jersey between 1786 and 1957; the largest was one of more than 10,000 coins found at La Marquanderie, St. Brelade, in 1935.

Roman coins have also been unearthed in both Jersey and Guernsey; a find of 357 coins was made in the former island in 1848 and another (at Rozel) in 1875. The most recent important find of coins in Jersey was at Le Câtillon de Haut, Grouville, in 1957. In Guernsey, Roman coins were found at St. Sampson's at the time when the foundations of the North Pier of the harbour were being prepared; other finds of Roman coins have been made at the Jerbourg Road and at Bordeaux.

For many centuries the recognized standard of money in the islands was the 'livre tournois', the coinage minted in the city of Tours in France. In Guernsey in 1553 Collas Guillemotte was authorized to make brass coinage; before then it appears that anyone was permitted to do so. In the early years of the nineteenth century tokens appeared in both bailiwicks. Three of these were in silver as follows: Guernsey—a 5s. token issued by Bishop de Jersey & Co. in 1809, which was forbidden to be circulated by Ordinance of 2nd October of the same year; Jersey—a 3s. token and an 18d. token issued by the States in 1811, both of which were withdrawn in 1834. In addition to the silver tokens a number of copper ones were issued in the islands during the early years of the nineteenth century. All these tokens were issued because of the shortage of coinage in circulation.

In Jersey a change was made from French to English currency in 1834. The pound sterling was equated to twenty-six livres tournois of twenty sous, each sous equal to one half-penny, thus resulting in a Jersey penny becoming one-thirteenth of a shilling British. In 1877 the position was regularized so that a Jersey penny and a British penny were on a parity. In Guernsey French currency remained legal tender until 1921. Before then twelve eight-doubles made up a Guernsey shilling, twenty-one of which were equivalent to a pound sterling.

Guernsey started issuing her own coinage in 1830, eleven years before Jersey. Until this century the coinage was limited to copper and bronze coins in denominations of one, two, four and eight doubles. Double is pronounced 'dooble', a word originating from the double liard, worth one-eighth of a penny. Guernsey's coinage, unlike Jersey's, does not bear the Sovereign's head, except for the 10s. piece issued in 1966 and the 25p piece issued in 1972. The arms of the Bailiwick appear on the obverse of all Guernsey coins, again with the exception of the 10s. piece. The denomination and the date appear on the reverse of all 'coppers'. In addition, from 1956 the Guernsey lily is depicted on the reverse side of the 'coppers', a lily with three blooms issuing from a single stem on the eight-doubles and a single bloom on the four-doubles; the Guernsey cow is depicted on the reverse of the threepence. From the same year the name Guernsey (which also appears on the reverse) is spelt in the English way and the 'coppers' are the same size as their British equivalents and not slightly larger as formerly. In 1935 500 eight-doubles bearing the date 1934 were issued specially burnished to commemorate the centenary of the 1834 issue of coinage and the Silver Jubilee of King George V. In 1966 a 10s. piece (square in shape but with rounded corners), a 3d. piece (heavier than that issued in 1956), an eight-double piece and a four-double piece, were issued to commemorate the nine hundredth anniversary of the Battle of Hastings. Guernsey's decimal coinage is in the same denominations as in Britain. The 10p piece and the 5p piece were issued in 1968; on the reverse of the former appears the Guernsey cow and on that of the latter the Guernsey lily. The 50p piece was issued in 1969 and on its reverse appears the Cap of Maintenance of the Dukes of Normandy. The three denominations in bronze were issued in 1971. On the reverse of the 2p piece is depicted the Sark windmill and on that of the 1p a gannet. A 25p piece was issued in 1972 to commemorate the Royal Silver Wedding.

Jersey issued her first copper coinage, consisting of a thirteenth, twenty-sixth and fifty-second of a shilling, in 1841. From then until the present day all the island's coinage has always borne the Sovereign's head on the obverse and the arms of the bailiwick on the reverse. From and including the issue of 1877, the denominations changed to a twelfth, twenty-fourth and forty-eighth of a shilling. Farthings ceased to be issued after 1877 and halfpence after 1947. In 1949 a 1*d.* piece was struck to commemorate the Liberation of the Island in 1945; a further issue of this coin was made in 1953, but with the head of Queen Elizabeth II on the obverse. In 1957 a new denomination, the 3*d.* piece or one-fourth of a shilling, was introduced. In 1960 a 1*d.* piece was issued to commemorate the tercentenary of the Restoration of King Charles II. In 1965 a 5*s.* piece, a 3*d.* piece and a penny were issued to commemorate the nine-hundredth anniversary of the Battle of Hastings. Jersey's decimal coinage is in the same denominations as in Britain. The 10p piece and the 5p piece were issued in 1968 to be followed by the 50p piece in 1969. The three denominations in bronze were issued in 1971. Jersey commemorated the Royal Silver Wedding by issuing a set of nine gold and silver coins ranging from £50 to 50p.

The history of bank-notes in the Channel Islands goes back further than the regular issues of coinage. Jersey's note issues commenced with that of Hugh Godfray in 1797; from then until the present day dozens of issues have been made, the latest regular one being that of the States in denominations of £10, £5 and £1. Private and parochial issues have long ceased. During the German Occupation the States issued £65,000 worth of notes in denominations of £1, 10*s.*, 2*s.* (two issues), 1*s.* and 6*d.* With the exception of the first 2*s.* note, they were all designed by the local artist, Edmund Blampied; the printer of the whole series was J. T. Bigwood Ltd. The States of Guernsey started issuing notes in 1816 and have continued doing so ever since. The present issue is in denominations of £5 and £1. The designs of the current issue of each bailiwick are most attractive.

Medals
From time to time medals have been struck to commemorate people and events connected either with Jersey or Guernsey. Some of these, such as coronation medals, are of little interest, but there are others of special interest and worthy of mention.

The oldest of these is the Tupper Medal and Chain, both of gold, presented by King William III and Queen Mary II to Jean Tupper in 1692 for signal service rendered before the battle of La Hogue. It would appear that Tupper, who commanded the privateer *Monmouth Galley*, was crossing in his vessel from Guernsey to England when he spied the French fleet through the fog and, proceeding with all haste to Spithead, informed the Admiral there of the Frenchmen's presence. The Tupper Medal and Chain are on permanent loan to the Lukis and Island Museum, St. Peter Port, but for security reasons only a replica is on display; the Tupper Portrait in which Jean Tupper is shown wearing the medal and chain is also on permanent loan to the same museum.

A medal comparing in magnificence with the Tupper Medal was that awarded by Queen Anne to a Jerseyman, James Lemprière (born 1654), Captain R.N., for services rendered in 1703 when he successfully conducted the squadron commanded by Rear-Admiral Dilkes to destroy a considerable number of French merchant ships which were in convoy off their own coast between Avranches and Mont St. Michel. On the obverse of the medal appear the head and shoulders of the Queen and on the reverse an inscription stating the reason for the award and depicting the Lemprière Arms, with the inscription "True to my Trust" beneath them.

Another famous Guernsey medal is that awarded by Major-General Small, the Lieutenant-Governor, to Jean Breton for services rendered as a pilot in 1794. In June of that year that famous Guernseyman, Captain Sir James de Saumarez (later Lord de Saumarez), was at Plymouth when he was ordered to proceed with his squadron of three ships to Guernsey and Jersey to discover the French naval strength at St. Malo and Cancale Bay. A few days prior to sailing de Saumarez met Breton and discovering that he was awaiting a passage to Guernsey offered to take him across. A day after setting sail the British squadron encountered a considerably superior French force some miles north-north-west of Guernsey, and, as it was impossible to engage the enemy at such a numerical disadvantage, de Saumarez wished to withdraw his own ships to safety. He first covered the escape of the *Eurydice* and the *Druid* to Guernsey and then made as though to run his own ship, the *Crescent*, on to the rocks. In fact he was relying on Breton to pilot the vessel through the dangerous rocks by a passage never previously negotiated by a ship of that size. Those who watched from the Guernsey shore did so anxiously for they thought that the *Crescent* would inevitably strike the rocks, not knowing that such a skilful pilot was aboard. The hazardous manoeuvre was successfully accomplished, and the *Crescent* and her gallant commander and crew were soon safely out of the enemy's reach. At the most dangerous moment of the exploit de Saumarez asked Breton if he was sure of his marks, to which he received the now famous reply, "Quite sure, for there is your house and yonder is my own!" The medal is preserved in the Guille-Allès Museum, St. Peter Port.

On 4th June 1804 smoke was observed issuing from the vent-holes of the powder magazine on the Mont de la Ville, St. Helier. The Signals Officer, Philip Lys (1763–1826), was informed and taking with him Edward Touzel (1782–1815), a carpenter, and William Penteney, a private of the 31st Regiment, ran to the magazine. Touzel broke into the building and brought out several chests of powder and threw out quantities of burning fuses, which Lys and Penteney removed to a safe distance; water was then fetched and the fire put out. In recognition of their brave conduct the States voted a sum of money to Lys and Touzel, an annuity to Penteney, and a gold medal to each of them. Touzel was promoted to Sergeant-Major in the Town Battalion of the Militia and presented with a silver-mounted sword, which he was authorized to wear. He also received a gift from the parish of St. Helier. A replica, in base metal, of Touzel's medal is in the museum, St. Helier.

The royal visit to Jersey in 1846 was commemorated by the issue of a large medallion depicting on the obverse the arrival of Queen Victoria and Prince Albert at St. Helier's Harbour; on the reverse is an inscription within a wreath.

A medal was issued in 1863 to commemorate the unveiling of the Prince Consort's statue at the top of the Albert Pier, St. Peter Port (see Chapter VII) on 8th October of that year. It is $1\frac{1}{2}$ inches in diameter, $\frac{1}{8}$ inch thick and has raised edges. The obverse shows the statue with the name Guernsey beneath; the reverse shows a laurel wreath within which is the legend "In Remembrance of Albert the Good, 1863". One of these medals is in the Guille-Allès Museum, St. Peter Port.

Prizewinners at the Channel Islands Exhibition of 1871 were

awarded large medals with a design on one side denoting commerce and plenty and on the other the arms of Jersey and Guernsey and the date within a border inscribed "Channel Islands Exhibition * Prize Medal".

The centenary of the introduction of Wesleyan Methodism into the Channel Islands was marked by the issue of a commemorative medal in 1884, depicting John Wesley and inscribed with the names de Quetteville, Clarke, Wesley, Brackenbury and Coke.

Heraldry

The Channel Islands are interesting heraldically, despite the fact that many of the arms borne by insular families have never been registered with the College of Heralds in London.

The arms of the Bailiwicks of Jersey and Guernsey are derived from the Royal Arms on the seal given to the bailiffs in 1279 (see Chapter V) for the authentication of documents. In course of time and without authority the bailiwicks adopted the Royal Arms (three golden lions—sometimes called leopards—passant-guardant palewise on a red ground) as their own, but the position was regularized by King Edward VII in 1907. The single and very minor difference between the arms of the two bailiwicks is the sprig appearing above the Guernsey Arms. The arms of Alderney are derived from the seal purchased for the Court in 1745. They consist of a golden crowned lion holding in its right fore paw a sprig (identified variously as holly, laurel or olive), the whole against a green ground. The arms of Sark are also derived from the Island's seal. They are, in fact, the arms of the de Carteret family—four silver lozenges joined at their points, against a red ground, the shield surmounted by a crest consisting of a brown squirrel sitting on a green mound cracking a brown nut, and supported by two winged red deer with blue tongues.

The badges used by the Jersey parishes were designed by the late Major N. V. L. Rybot, a well-known local heraldic expert, in or before 1923, and have been gradually adopted officially by the parochial authorities; they were not inspired by any previous parish emblems and were pure invention on the part of Major Rybot. Hanging in the King's Arcade (commonly called de Gruchy's Arcade), St. Helier, are twelve shields on each of which is painted one of the parish badges in its correct colours.

Arms are featured in the parish churches and on tombstones in the parochial and other cemeteries; as well as in Gorey Castle and Elizabeth Castle, Jersey; Castle Cornet, Guernsey; on the Royal Court Houses, on old houses, and in many other places; also on silver plate, both ecclesiastical and secular.

There was once an officer of the College of Heralds called Mont Orgueil, who almost certainly derived his name from Mont Orgueil Castle in Jersey. There has been only one known holder of the title, first as a pursuivant, in the reigns of King Henry VII and King Henry VIII. Randulph Jackson, alias Mont Argule, was appointed around 1494; he was promoted Herald by Patent in 1516, still being called Mont Argule, and granted twenty marks a year. Jackson's christian name appeared sometimes as Randle and his surname as Holmes. He became Chester Herald by Patent in 1533. He appears to have vanished from the scene in 1545.

John Gibbon, who became Bluemantle Herald in 1668, visited Jersey in 1655 when his cousin, Colonel Robert Gibbon, was the Governor (see Chapter IV), and recorded a number of coats of arms.

Flags

In Jersey the Union Jack is flown from the flagstaff on the western bastion of Fort Regent. By tradition the flag is never half-masted except on the death of the Sovereign. The lieutenant-governor of each bailiwick has his official flag, which is the Union Jack with the arms of the Bailiwick at its centre. In Jersey it is flown from the flagstaff in the grounds of Government House at all times when His Excellency is in the island; it is never half-masted unless the lieutenant-governor dies and is only hauled down when he leaves the island or vacates his appointment. The flag is also flown on the bonnet of the lieutenant-governor's motor car when he is travelling about the island and from the masthead of any ship in which he embarked. Similar remarks apply to Guernsey.

The Jersey flag is the cross of St. Patrick, which is described heraldically as a saltire gules on a field argent. The insular colours of red and white are presumably derived from those of the flag. It would appear that the cross of St. Patrick became the Jersey flag as the result of the mis-reading of an entry in an eighteenth-century book of charts. It is not possible to prove the adoption of the flag before about 1841. The Guernsey flag is the cross of St. George, but how long it has been so is a matter for conjecture; its continued use as the distinctive flag of the island was specifically approved by King Edward VIII in 1936.

During the German Occupation the Jersey and Guernsey flags were used at sea, notably on the M.V. *White Heather* on the Guernsey–Sark service and on S.S. *Normand* and certain other vessels plying between Jersey, France (Granville) and Guernsey.

By an Admiralty Warrant of 1907 authorization was given for the Blue Ensign with the arms of Jersey in the fly, and a jack of similar design to be worn on board the steam-tug *Duke of Normandy*. The arms on the ensign and jack are in the centre of the fly, and contained within circles. The authorization contained in the warrant was limited to the one vessel, and it has been necessary for the States to obtain a renewed authorization to use the same ensign and jack on their two present vessels.

By an Admiralty Warrant of 1894, authorization was given for the Blue Ensign with the distinctive marks of the Royal Channel Islands Yacht Club to be worn on board respective vessels belonging to the club and to its members, subject to conditions. The club burgee is blue and bears the Jersey Arms surmounted by the Crown; the ensign is blue and bears the same distinctive marks. The commodore's flag is the club burgee swallow-tailed; the vice-commodore's flag is the same, but with a white ball in the upper corner; the rear-commodore's has two white balls in the upper corner.

In 1952 the Admiralty gave permission for the St. Helier Yacht Club to fly a defaced Red Ensign in recognition of the service rendered by its members in evacuating troops and demolition squads from St. Malo in 1940; the defacing takes the form of two crossed axes of gold on a blue ground (the badge of the parish of St. Helier) and an anchor; these emblems also feature on the club's burgee. At one time the Channel Islands were important shipping centres and many of the shipowners had their house flags.

Alderney's flag was approved by Edward VII in 1906. It is the same as Guernsey's except that it has the arms of Alderney at its centre.

The Lordship of Sark has its own flag, which is the cross of St. George with two golden lions passant-guardant on a red ground occupying the whole of the top left-hand corner.

The colours of Guernsey are green and white and those of Alderney blue and white; Sark has no colours.

Postal History

Prior to 1794 there were no regular British post offices in the Channel Islands. Letters were entrusted to the care of travellers or to the captains of ships and were deposited with merchants and others, who acted as unofficial post offices. Although adhesive postage stamps did not exist, from at least as early as 1683 markings were used on some of this mail.

By Act of Parliament post offices were established in both Jersey and Guernsey in 1794. Jersey's first postmaster was Captain Charles William Le Geyt (1733–1827), who was appointed in 1794 and held the position until 1815, when at the age of 82 years he retired in favour of his son, George William Le Geyt. The first postmaster in Guernsey was in fact a postmistress, in the person of Mrs. Ann Watson, who was appointed the same year as Captain Le Geyt. She was a relative of Paul Le Mesurier, Lord Mayor of London. Like the first Jersey postmaster, she was succeeded by her son, Nicholas Watson. A post office was established in Alderney in 1843 and in Sark in 1857; Herm had an official post office from 1925 to 1938.

Just as the first postmaster in Guernsey was a woman, so the first letter carrier, or postman, in Jersey was a woman in the person of Mary Godfray, who was appointed in 1798. She was the only letter carrier in the island from that year until 1830. It is said that she divided the letters for delivery into two bundles, one of which she placed in a red pocket handkerchief and the other in a blue one.

In 1852 the first four street letter-boxes erected by the Post Office in the British Isles were installed in St. Helier at the instance of Anthony Trollope, the famous Victorian novelist, who was also a Post Office Surveyor. The centenary of this event was marked by the unveiling by the Postmaster-General of a new pillar-box, surmounted by a commemorative plaque, near the Cheapside entrance of the Parade Gardens in St. Helier. In 1853 three letter-boxes were erected in Guernsey. Unfortunately the design of these Channel Islands' boxes has not been preserved, although it is known that they were made locally by a John Vaudin.

Because they did not issue postage stamps, the Channel Islands were for a long time of no interest to stamp collectors, except for a small minority who specialized in postal history. However, with the coming of the German Occupation the islands came into their own philatelically because during those dark years they issued their own stamps for the first time. Guernsey had three denominations—$\frac{1}{2}d$., $1d$. and $2\frac{1}{2}d$.—in different printings and on various papers; Jersey at first issued two denominations—$\frac{1}{2}d$. and $1d$.—followed later by a pictorial set made up of six denominations—$\frac{1}{2}d$., $1d$., $1\frac{1}{2}d$., $2d$., $2\frac{1}{2}d$. and $3d$.—all designed by Edmund Blampied and printed in Paris.

After the Liberation, the bi-sects (i.e. British twopenny stamps cut in two and used as penny ones) and occupation issues attracted attention among philatelists, some of whom began to take an interest in the islands. This interest was stimulated first by the Liberation issue of 1948 and secondly by the regional issues for each bailiwick which first appeared in 1958. The $2\frac{1}{2}d$. of the Liberation issue was from a drawing by Edmund Blampied, who also designed the same denomination (1964) for the Jersey regional issue.

With the setting up of the Insular Postal Administrations and the first issues of stamps on 1st October 1969, the islands became firmly established in the philatelic world. To mark the occasion Jersey issued a commemorative set of four denominations. Guernsey's first commemorative issue was made on 1st December 1969, to mark the bi-centenary of the birth of Major-General Sir Isaac Brock, Governor of Upper Canada.

Jersey and Guernsey also issue revenue stamps. Local stamps were issued in Sark, Brechou, Herm, Jethou and Lihou, but these have been discontinued since the States of Guernsey assumed responsibility for postal services within the bailiwick.

Food and Drink

As in most other places, the Channel Islands had their own specialities in both food and drink, of which the ingredients were for the most part locally produced. Most of the traditional dishes have disappeared or are rarely to be met with.

One associates the Channel Islands with seafood. Pride of place in this category must go to the ormer, or ear of the sea (*Haliotis tuberculata*), for, although it is found elsewhere, it does not venture further north than the islands. The ormer is unattractive to look at either in or out of its shell. However, the interior of the shell is attractive, resembling mother-of-pearl. Families who are accustomed to eating ormers have their own recipes for preparing and cooking this delicacy, and there are slight variations from household to household, each claiming their method to be the best. There are those who regard the preparation of ormers for the table as an arduous chore, but there are others—the true devotees—who look upon it as a pleasant ritual to be lovingly performed, upon the thoroughness of which depends future gastronomic pleasure. Briefly, the preparation consists of removing the ormers from their shells, scrubbing and beating them, and then rubbing them with flour. They are then placed in a frying-pan with butter, at which time they much resemble steak. After frying until brown, they are put into a stew-pan or casserole with a small piece of pork or bacon and seasoning and cooked until tender, which takes some hours. There are many other piscatorial delights such as lobsters, crayfish, crabs (the large ones are known in Jersey as Guernsey crabs or chankers), spider crabs, prawns and shrimps, to mention but a few. Undoubtedly, the best place for fish anywhere in the islands is the fish market in St. Peter Port—on a good day it is a splendid sight, a veritable harvest of the sea.

Channel Islands' milk, cream and butter are all first-class and play their part in the production of some of the local delicacies. In Jersey a preserve known as black butter was made from apples and cider which was spread on bread in the same way as butter. In the old days black butter was made in large quantities on a communal basis at convivial gatherings known as black butter nights; nowadays it is still made by a few people but on a very modest scale.

Neither the jersey nor the guernsey are beef cattle, although their meat can be eaten. Locally produced pork, however, is highly considered.

A pig's trotter or a piece of pork is one of the ingredients in the traditional bean jar, still a favourite with Channel Islanders. The other ingredients of this very tasty dish are dried beans, which give it its name, onions and herbs. The beans are soaked overnight and then placed in an earthenware jar, covered with water and brought to the boil and then simmered for about eight hours. Originally this was a breakfast dish eaten on Sundays.

Soups of various kinds were also popular in the islands. One which has survived is conger soup, made out of the head of a conger eel boiled in milk, with marigold leaves and petals added.

Different sorts of cakes were also popular in the islands. That known as Guernsey *gâche* (a fruit dough cake) is produced in large quantities by the island's cake shops. Another local speciality still in evidence is the Guernsey biscuit, which is not really a biscuit, but is round and flat and is of a consistency similar to that of a soft roll.

There are three Jersey Easter dishes—fiottes, simnels and wonders. The first named are made from self-raising flour, sugar and eggs, to which a pinch of salt is added. The mixture is rolled into balls which are cooked in milk. The fact that they float on the boiling liquid gives them their name of *fiottes* (floats). Simnels are the subject of an old Jersey saying: "It is not Easter without simnels." Formerly they were available in large quantities, many a baker's window being piled high with them, but very few are now made. The Jersey simnel, a sort of bowl-shaped biscuit made from flour, sugar, eggs and butter, is first boiled and then baked in a very hot oven and bears no resemblance to the English simnel cake. The Jersey wonder, which tastes like a doughnut without the jam, is still manufactured commercially and at home. It is a dough cake in the shape of a twisted figure eight and is made from flour, sugar, eggs and butter, then cooked in deep lard until brown, and eaten cold. Just as each household has its own recipe for cooking ormers, so it has for making wonders. It is said by some that they should never be cooked on a rising tide for if they are the fat will boil over!

All the old time Channel Islands' drinks have virtually disappeared, except for a small amount of local cider which is still produced.

Weights and Measures

The legal standard of weight in the Channel Islands was the *poids de marc de Rouen* and that for measuring liquids and corn was the *Etalon du Chasteau*; there were also local land measures. In Jersey all the local weights and measures, with the exception of land measures, were abolished in 1917. Land is still referred to in *vergées*, two and a quarter of which equal one English acre. In contracts relating to the transfer of property, measurements of area are quoted in Jersey measure, but measurements of distance, e.g. between boundary stones, are quoted in English feet. The Guernsey *vergée* is smaller than the Jersey *vergée*, two and a half

Coins: (top) *reverse of 1830 double, reverse of 1966 10s., reverse of 1956 3d.* (bottom) *obverse of 1834 eight doubles, reverse of 1968 five new pence, obverse of 1968 ten new pence*

being equivalent to one English acre. The old Jersey standard measures of capacity and standard weights formerly in the care of the Viscount are now deposited in the museum, St. Helier; the five Guernsey standard measures, cast in bronze in 1615, and formerly in the care of the Sheriff, together with the branding irons and punches used to certify the correctness of other measures and two small nests of weights, were deposited in the Lukis and Island Museum, St. Peter Port, as were the wooden measures, formerly used by the Receiver-General to measure Crown rents payable in kind.

Francis Le Poidevin of Guernsey with his prize-winning crop of tomatoes

X

CATTLE AND CROPS

The soil sufficiently fertile in itself,
but most curiously manured, and of a
plentifull increase unto the Barn.
Peter Heylyn (1600–62)

Jersey and Guernsey are famous for their cattle and agricultural produce, potatoes and tomatoes from Jersey, and grapes, tomatoes and flowers from Guernsey. Nowadays, Jersey is concentrating more on the growing of flowers, while Guernsey's grape industry is on the decline. Jersey also exports cauliflowers.

One reason for Jersey and Guernsey being so well-known throughout large areas of the world is because of their cattle which have spread far and wide. Outside their native Islands jerseys and guernseys have to compete with many other breeds, but at home they have been protected by legislation; since 1789 no live cattle have been allowed in Jersey other than jerseys, and once one of the breed is exported it is not permitted to return; similar legislation has applied in Guernsey for very many years although the enactment at present in force dates only from 1952. Incidentally, it should be noted that guernseys are the sole cattle on Alderney and Sark. There is no Alderney breed, despite the fact that in time past Channel Islands' cattle were often referred to indiscriminately as alderneys.

It has been suggested that Jersey cattle are derived from no fewer than four sources, and it has been said that undoubtedly the mulberry jersey has a close connection with the old cattle of the Normandy and Brittany coastal districts. The characteristics of a guernsey are also to be seen in jerseys, and *vice versa*; this results from the fact that long ago when the daughter of a Guernsey farmer married a Jerseyman she took with her a calf as part of her dowry, and the same applied in reverse. There is quite a considerable variation in colour among jerseys, but they are generally a pleasant shade of fawn. The cows and calves are exceedingly beautiful animals.

Guernsey cattle are larger than Jersey cattle and would seem to have originated from a cross between the Froment de Léon, a breed common to the area around the town of St. Pol de Léon in Brittany, and the Isigny breed from Normandy. Both breeds were almost certainly introduced into Guernsey by the monks many centuries ago.

In the Channel Islands the cattle are often found tethered, although not as much as formerly. When tethered, they have to be moved several times a day. The herds are small compared with many in the United Kingdom. In both bailiwicks great care is exercised in preserving standards and herd books are maintained recording the pedigrees of all registered cattle. Both jerseys and guernseys produce a large quantity of milk with a high butterfat content. Butter produced from the milk is of a bright yellow colour.

At this point it is appropriate to refer to the old Channel Islands' milkcans, which are unlike any in the United Kingdom, although they are said to resemble the old milkcans of Brittany. The Jersey can varies slightly in detail from the Guernsey one, but apart they are indistinguishable to the casual observer. It would seem that in Guernsey this type of milkcan was introduced in 1796 by J. Noel, who made them at 17 Market Street, St. Peter Port, a property now demolished. One firm which continues to make these cans, now almost exclusively sold as souvenirs, is directly descended from the Noel business. The cans were made in fifteen sizes, the largest holding 40 pints. The largest one made today holds 24 pints. The design is supposed to be such that the can has the largest capacity using the minimum of metal. The high neck prevents the milk from slopping over and the lid always fits tightly to prevent dust from entering. Milkcans are also made in Jersey.

At one time numerous sheep were to be found on the islands. They were almost exclusively confined to the commons and to rough pasture unsuitable for other livestock. Nowadays they have practically disappeared, although some are still kept on Sark and a few on Guernsey.

Originally the arable land on the islands was cultivated in open strips, but in course of time these were enclosed by hedges into the innumerable small fields which exist today. The land itself is variable, ranging from sand to clay and stone to marsh. Until the advent of chemical fertilizers, natural manure, especially *vraic* (seaweed) was used on the land.

For centuries seaweed has been used in the Channel Islands for manuring the land and is still used for that purpose, but to a far lesser extent than formerly. In time past, vraicing was carried out on a tremendous scale and numerous vraicers, carts and even boats were employed to gather the harvest. The times of the year when *vraic* could be gathered were officially laid down, as they still are. So eager were the *vraic* gatherers to obtain all they could that they would sometimes remain on the beach until the carts were floating and the horses swimming; they even carted the precious seaweed on their backs up cliff sides. The traditional vraicing carts are no longer seen, although the Jersey four-pronged forks and the vraicing hooks survive. Whereas nowadays fresh *vraic* is spread on the land as manure, in time past it was sometimes burnt and the ashes spread on the land. *Vraic* burning was traditionally carried on at St. Ouen in Jersey, and as those engaged in the work used to get covered in grey dust, they were given the nickname of grey bellies. Generally, farmers collected their own *vraic*, but there were some, as there are today, who gathered seaweed as an occupation. In the vicinity of La Pulente at the southern end of St. Ouen's Bay in Jersey are to be seen stacks of *vraic*, which are sold by the gatherers for some pounds a piece. The sight of a horse pulling a cart dripping with newly gathered *vraic*, rich brown and glistening, and with a *vraic* fork or two sticking out from the back of the load, has gone forever, as also the sound of cartwheels rumbling over the granite setts of a slipway. Fortunately, such a sight has been preserved not only in photographs, but more especially in the etchings and paintings of Edmund Blampied; so well has he depicted the subject that on looking at his vraicing scenes it is almost possible to smell the salt in one's nostrils. It should be mentioned also that dried *vraic* was at one time used for fuel.

Guernsey is famous for its grapes, great luscious fruit, surpassing all other grapes more commonly met with. The industry is something like a century and a quarter old. In the early years Jersey produced even more grapes than Guernsey, but for some reason their cultivation in that island on a commercial scale declined and ultimately ceased. Unfortunately, even in Guernsey the grape-growing industry is on the decline and many glass-houses originally intended for the growing of vines are now given over to the growing of the all-pervading tomato.

Jersey new potatoes are famous. The potato has been grown as a field crop in the island since some time in the second half of the eighteenth century and has been exported since the early years of the nineteenth. In 1807 some 600 tons were sent out of the island and by 1811 the amount exported had more than doubled to 1,400 tons. A stimulus was given to the potato industry around 1880 when Hugh de la Haye (1835–1906) introduced the Royal Jersey Fluke, commonly known as 'the Royal'. By 1891 the quantity of potatoes exported from Jersey had risen to 66,840 tons worth £487,642; in the late 1960s the quantity had dropped to some 42,000 tons worth more than £3,320,000.

In the past, more than nowadays, the potato season was part of Jersey's way of life. Local labour was augmented by French labour, particularly from Brittany. The Breton women in their black dresses, coifs and wooden sabots added a picturesque touch to the local scene. French workers still come, but, sadly, their dress is no longer distinctive. The term 'complete fork' used in connection with the potato harvest, means a team of three workers—a digger, a picker and a shaker.

Those who buy Jersey new potatoes in the United Kingdom have little idea of how they can really taste. The best place to eat them is in Jersey when they have been freshly dug, washed, scraped and boiled in a saucepan with a sprig of mint—then they are truly delicious.

As Jersey is associated with the growing of potatoes, so Guernsey is with the growing of tomatoes. There is little doubt that the tomato was grown there originally as a decorative plant which produced 'love apples'. The date when it was first grown commercially in that island is not precisely known, but it is thought to have been around 1874. This new industry must have got off to a good start, for by 1893 a writer on the islands stated that: "The cultivation of tomatoes under glass has lately become a large industry in Guernsey." In the late 1960s just under 50,000 tons of tomatoes, worth nearly £9,250,000, were exported annually. The tomato has changed the face of the Guernsey countryside, for it has been the cause of the building of a large acreage of glasshouses.

Although Guernsey is particularly famous for the growing of tomatoes, Jersey also has a substantial tomato industry. Whereas Guernsey grows her tomatoes in glasshouses, Jersey grows the bulk of hers out of doors. Jersey's tomato industry is somewhat younger than that of her neighbour; nevertheless, it is substantial, and by the late 1960s over 20,000 tons were exported annually worth over £1,870,000.

For some years Jersey has been growing cauliflowers (those produced in winter are called broccoli) on a commercial scale, and these are exported in large quantities. In the late 1960s some 16,500 tons were exported annually worth about £750,000.

Both Jersey and Guernsey produce large quantities of flowers for export. As with the tomato, Guernsey was first in the field. The industry in that island can be said to date from 1864 when a single consignment of daffodils was sent to the London market by Charles Smith of the Caledonia Nursery; this was a few years earlier than the first consignment from the Scilly Isles. The industry has developed considerably from that modest beginning, and by the late 1960s nearly 5,000 tons of flowers, worth nearly £3,350,000, were being exported annually. Jersey's flower industry, although it was started later than Guernsey's, has made great strides, and by the late 1960s some 1,825 tons, worth nearly £1,000,000, were exported annually.

Few places of the same size and population as the Channel Islands possess as many agricultural societies. Of the many in Jersey mention should be made of the Royal Jersey Agricultural Society, which was founded in 1833 and was the successor of the Jersey Agricultural Society founded in 1790, it was made a 'Royal' society in 1834. Of the societies in Guernsey mention should be made of the Royal Guernsey Agricultural and Horticultural Society, founded in 1842; like its opposite number in Jersey, it was the successor of an earlier society founded in 1817. Soon after the new society was established Queen Victoria consented to become its patroness, and it has been under royal patronage ever since. In Alderney there is the Royal Alderney Agricultural Society, and in Sark the Garden and Farm Produce Show Committee, Cattle Show Committee and the Horse Show Committee.

XI

TOURISM AND ENTERTAINMENT

Many people think that tourism is a modern industry in the Channel Islands. Nothing is further from the truth. In the days of the Grand Tour the Channel Islands were not considered important enough to form part of the itinerary, but by the late eighteenth century a few people were going to see what they were like. However, it was when peace had descended on Europe, following the defeat of Napoleon I in 1815, that the tourist industry really started.

The islands first became well-known because of the large number of residents, to begin with almost exclusively retired British naval and army officers, who settled there owing to the comparative cheapness of living. 'The residents', as such people were (and are still) called, were visited by friends and relations, and this resulted in the islands becoming still better known, until they were finally recognized as tourist resorts in the late 1820s or early 1830s. At first just a trickle of visitors made its way to the islands, but as the century advanced this trickle became a steady flow, and when the nineteenth century gave way to the twentieth the flow increased with the passing of the years until now, when over a million holidaymakers visit the islands every year.

From early in the nineteenth century, guide-books to Jersey, Guernsey and the Channel Islands in general began to make their appearance. Some of these publications were directed more to intending 'residents' than to visitors. One of the earliest was *A Picture of Jersey* by J. Stead, published in London in 1809; another, *A Summer Stroll through the Islands of Jersey and Guernsey*, was published in Jersey in 1811. Some guide-books—such as *The Channel Islands* by H. D. Inglis, first published in London in 1834 —went into a number of editions, and are substantial works giving good contemporary accounts of the islands.

Another reason for the Channel Islands developing as tourist resorts after 1815 was that crossing the English Channel no longer involved the hazard of a possible encounter with the enemy, as it had done previously, and also that communications were continually improving. The sailing packets and other vessels of the early years of the century soon gave way to steam packets and paddle-steamers and later to the steamers belonging to the railway companies of which the British Rail vessels *Caesarea* and *Sarnia* are the lineal descendants. In the 1930s communications were revolutionized by the introduction of air passenger services, and nowadays there are air services linking the islands with all parts of the United Kingdom, as well as with the Republic of Ireland and France; there are also inter-insular air services. Sea excursions between the islands and the neighbouring ports of France, namely St. Malo, Granville and Carteret, have always been popular, and during the summer months are made by boat and hydrofoil; there are also air excursions.

Because the islands' tourist industries are so long established, a number of the hotels date from as early as the first half of the nineteenth century and have a long tradition of good service to the visitor. Every effort is made by the authorities in all the islands to maintain high standards in hotel accommodation and the system of compulsory grading and inspection as obtaining in Jersey and Guernsey is the envy of other resorts. Whatever the formula employed by the islands in organizing the industry, it must satisfy the visitors, for many of them return year after year and some even reserve rooms at the end of one holiday for the next.

Travel within the islands, except for Sark, has changed a great deal since the old days. The majority of visitors to Jersey and Guernsey in the early nineteenth century would, generally speaking, have stayed either in St. Helier or St. Peter Port. If they wished to explore the island where they were staying they could travel on horseback, by carriage or by horse-drawn excursion car; the latter became very popular in Jersey and each car was accompanied by a guide who explained the points of interest during the drive. There were also, for a time, two railways in Jersey and a tramway in Guernsey (see Chapter XIII). Nowadays there are buses, coaches and hire cars to take the sightseers about, and some visitors bring their own cars with them.

Initially bathing was not much indulged in by the visitors (or by the islanders), who were more interested in scenery and sight-seeing than in disporting themselves in the sea; sun-bathing was unheard of. In these days it is amusing to read this "Direction for Sea-Bathing" which appeared in a guide-book to the islands published in 1833:

To those who are enjoined the use of sea-bathing, the following hints may not be unworthy of notice.

The most proper time for sea-bathing is early in the morning, before which no exercise ought to be taken; all previous fatigue tending to diminish that force, which the fibres when contracted will otherwise have, of removing obstructions more effectually—one of the great ends sought for in bathing.

To bathe late in the day, (more especially in hot weather), will occasion great depression of the spirits, particularly in debilitated or paralytic persons.

It is recommended on the morning fasting, repletion being very improper before going into the sea, as it counteracts one of the effects we aim to procure by sea-bathing.

Perfect repose of body and serenity of mind are equally suited to the use of this great remedy, giving it full force and efficacy.

It is impossible to pronounce absolutely with what particular constitutions and temperaments sea-bathing will, or will not agree; experience only can ascertain, when it is or is not proper to each individual respectively.

It may be said to agree perfectly, when soon after coming out of the sea the bathers find their spirits exhilarated, and feel an universal glow through the system.

When the contrary to this happens to any, it may reasonably be presumed that a further perseverance in bathing would be in some degree prejudicial to such persons, and that they should desist, at least for some time from it.

But as staying imprudently too long in the water, may sometimes occasion a temporary depression of the spirits, and bring on a chilliness or shivering for a time, a proper distinction must be observed between the use and abuse of the remedy, sea-water being by no means (either respecting its external or internal use), of an indifferent nature; when judiciously managed, it does much good; when unadvisedly and indiscriminately had recourse to, it may do much harm.

Sea-bathing is useful in those cases where the energy of the vital principle should be increased, and where the strength of the muscles should be augmented; it improves the appetite and promotes digestion.

The above "Direction" was written in an age very different from the present, when in summer the islands' beaches become covered with myriads of brown bodies clad in minimal costumes, who spend much of their time disporting themselves in the water as though they belonged to that element rather than to the land. Surf-bathing, skin-diving and water ski-ing may all be indulged in to the heart's content.

In former days Jersey sported several pleasure gardens; the first was Prince's Tower (now the property known as La Hougue Bie—see Chapter I) where there were a hotel with a skittle alley, and a gazebo (the tower which gave its name to the place) constructed above the old chapels on top of the mound. Old Pontac Hotel at St. Clement had gardens containing a maze that was a copy of the one at Hampton Court Palace. While at St. Saviour a wondrous pleasure garden known as the Troglodyte Caves was contrived by a Mr. Champion in a disused claypit. The so-called caves were covered with thousands of shells, and there was an artificial lake which was crossed by a miniature paddle-boat, the *Busy Bee*. On gala occasions the grounds were brilliantly illuminated. There was also a tropical garden at 'La Chaire', Rozel.

Nowadays there is a very wide range of 'pleasure gardens' and other attractions in the islands—with the exception of Sark, which still relies on its own unspoilt beauty. In addition to a number of beautiful parks, Jersey and Guernsey each has a small zoo—at Les Augrès Manor (see Chapter I), Trinity, in the former island and at La Villiaize, near the airport, in the latter. The two larger islands and Alderney have potteries where visitors may see the potters at work. The Jersey Pottery is at Gorey Village; the three in Guernsey are located respectively at Les Capelles, St. Sampson's; La Girouette, Grandes Rocques; and at Moulin Huet, St. Martin's. The Alderney Pottery is at La Trigale on the western side of St. Anne.

Jersey and Guernsey have each had a theatre for very many years; their present theatres are respectively the Opera House and the Little Theatre. Guernsey's first regular theatre was established around 1793–4 on a site in St. Peter Port now occupied by part of the Royal Court House. Possibly the most famous actor ever to have appeared there was Edmund Kean. Jersey's first regular playhouse, the Theatre Royal, was established in St. Helier in 1802. Before then travelling companies had visited the island and performed in the Long Room, above the Corn Market which was in the Market Place (now the Royal Square). A new theatre, also called Theatre Royal, was built in the centre of the Royal Crescent in 1828, but destroyed by fire in 1863. It was replaced by another Theatre Royal in 1865, this time situated in Gloucester Street. This was also destroyed by fire in 1899 and replaced by the present Opera House in 1900. That year, on 9th July, Lillie Langtry with her London company opened the new building with a performance of *The Degenerates*. At the conclusion of the play she made a short speech which she finished by reciting some lines in Jersey-French written by a local poet, her words bringing forth salvos of applause. The Opera House is still the only building used regularly in Jersey as a theatre, and each year a show is presented there during the summer season. Jersey and Guernsey have amateur theatrical societies—every year at Christmas the Jersey Green Room Club and the Guernsey Amateur Dramatic and Operatic Club each presents a pantomime.

A number of famous artistes have appeared on the stage of the Opera House, notably Mabel Love in 1906; Mrs. Patrick Campbell and Mark Hambourg, both in 1907; Charlie Chaplin with Fred Karno's Company in *The Mumming Birds* in 1912, Lady Little (20 years old, 23 inches tall, weight 10½ pounds) and Marie Lloyd in 1913. A newspaper review of *The Mumming Birds* stated that: "the initiation ceremony through which Mr. Chaplin had to go—well, Freemasonry can't be in it". It is said that during this visit to Jersey, Charlie Chaplin went to the Battle of Flowers and was filmed for the first time—by a cameraman who was covering the event.

In Jersey during the early years of the twentieth century concert parties were put on in the summer and performed, if the weather was fine, either in the Horseshoe Quarry or the Triangle Park; if it was wet they performed in West Park Pavilion (then nicknamed the Tin Hut owing to the fact that it had a corrugated iron roof), the forerunner of the present Pavilion (1931, by Roy Blampied). Two of the best-known of these troupes were the White Coon Banjo Team and the Gaieties. Two local songs popular at the time were "Beautiful Jersey", words and music by Lindsay

Lennox, and *Sarnia Chérie* (Dearest Guernsey), words by G. A. Deighton and music by D. Santangelo. A traditional song, popular in Guernsey in the years gone by, was "Jean, Gros Jean".

Since the resumption of tourism in the islands after World War II, floor shows have become popular in both Jersey and Guernsey, and a number of cabarets are presented each year in the hotels and nightspots.

The Channel Islands have not retained their old dances such as Mon Bon Laurier, La Violette, La Bébée and La Bérouaïse (the last three are associated with Guernsey). It is in fact doubtful if dancing was as popular in the islands in the sixteenth and seventeenth centuries as elsewhere, owing to the puritanical views of the inhabitants. However, with the increasing prosperity of the late eighteenth century, coupled with the presence of a garrison in each island, assemblies (which would now be called dances) were held, and in the winter of 1782 subscription assembly rooms were opened in Guernsey. The original subscribers and their families together with the naval and army officers stationed in the island were dubbed the 'Sixties'; those with newly acquired wealth and who aspired to social position, but who were not of the 'Sixties', were dubbed the 'Forties' and excluded from the rooms. As a result of this, great bitterness was engendered similar to that which existed between the supporters of the Laurel and Rose political parties in Jersey (see Chapter V). Some of the rules observed in the Assembly Rooms at St. Peter Port, now part of the Guille-Allès Library, make amusing reading today and are worth quoting:

RULES OF THE PRIVATE ASSEMBLIES

1st. The Assemblies to take place every Tuesday (now altered to every other Tuesday) during the season; to open at seven, and to close at half-past eleven. The drawing of tickets to commence at half-past seven, the first numbers to be drawn by the ladies present, the remaining numbers to be drawn indiscriminately as the ladies come in.

2nd. No exchange of numbers permitted. Ladies losing tickets, stand at the bottom; if more than one, they draw for places.

3rd. As soon as drawing has taken place, dancing to commence with a quadrille, not exceeding five figures, which, with an English country dance, compose one set.

4th. Ladies sitting down during a dance, to stand at the bottom during the remainder of the evening.

5th. Officers in uniform are admitted in boots, but must not dance in spurs.

7th. No native inhabitant, whose parents have not previously subscribed, to be admitted, unless proposed by the Master of the Ceremonies, and approved of by two-thirds of the ladies and gentlemen subscribers present. None but native inhabitants entitled to vote.

9th. Every native inhabitant subscriber is liable to serve the office of Master of the Ceremonies, or find a deputy, under the penalty of 10s. 6d.

Ballroom dancing is not as popular as it once was, although 'pop' dancing has a big following. When Jersey's West Park Pavilion was rebuilt it was considered the ultimate as a ballroom. Today, like so much else, ballroom dancing has changed, dance floors have tended to get smaller and dance bands have been replaced by groups (with or without electronic organs) who beat out the current pop tunes with zest, causing a forest of feet to twitch and twirl in crazy choreography.

Nowadays the tourist season starts at Easter and then slackens off until Whitsun, when it gains momentum and continues without slackening until the end of September—even into October if the weather is good. It can be safely said that there are a few visitors in Jersey at almost all times of the year. The majority come from the United Kingdom and the Republic of Ireland. They reach the islands by plane, boat and car-ferry—in the case of Sark the last part of the journey has to be made by sea. At weekends especially the harbours and airports present scenes of intense activity. The islands are also visited by a large number of yachtsmen, and to cater for these Guernsey has established a yacht marina at Beaucette Quarry.

Most visitors, whatever else they may do, spend a large part of their time lazing and bathing on the islands' innumerable beaches. Although there are excursions between the islands, and between the islands and France, the vast majority are content to remain on the island of their choice. Those who like a more restful and care-free holiday go to Alderney, Sark or Herm; those who want somewhere with more life prefer Jersey or Guernsey.

Throughout the summer the towns of St. Helier and St. Peter Port are thronged each morning of the week with gaily dressed holidaymakers who crowd the narrow pavements gazing at the shop windows, especially those which display spirits, liqueurs, cigarettes, tobacco and cosmetics at local prices, far below those obtaining in the United Kingdom. The tea-rooms, where splendid cream pastries and cream teas can be obtained, are also filled to capacity. The circulation of traffic becomes a problem, and traffic jams are not infrequent. In the afternoon the visitors generally relax in one of the bays, take a coach trip or visit some of the many places of interest to be found in both Jersey and Guernsey. The evening is often spent in one of the many establishments providing either food, drink or entertainment, or a combination of all three. Restaurants are numerous and cater for all purses. Sometimes a public house is passed where a singsong is in progress, and the words of some famous song drift into the night air.

During the summer months the islands are as alive by night as they are by day. At night coloured lights fringe Havre des Pas and St. Aubin's Bay in Jersey; Gorey Castle and Elizabeth Castle in the same island and Castle Cornet in Guernsey are all floodlit. The shops of St. Helier and St. Peter Port are brightly lit and electric signs proclaim in brilliant colours the names of hotels, restaurants and public houses. As the season advances so the pace quickens until with August the crescendo is reached, with Battle of Flowers week in Jersey marking the height of the season.

From then on departures exceed arrivals, and the season slowly dies away. Gradually the hotels and boarding houses begin to close as do the seasonal restaurants and cafés; the floor shows give their final performances; the souvenir shops close and the unsold stocks are packed away. The sun begins to lose its warmth, and a chilly breeze, particularly in the evening, proclaims that autumn is on the way. Another season is over and the islands resume their ordinary routine. The seasonal workers return home—to Austria, Germany, France, Switzerland, Italy, Spain or Portugal—and the local people engaged in the tourist industry (as well as the farmers) start taking their holidays. Soon they will be home again and Christmas will be on the way. Plans are then made and work put in hand for yet another season; once more advertisements and brochures will invite potential holidaymakers to visit those "pieces of France fallen into the sea"—the Channel Islands.

One of the pleasures enjoyed by visitors is to take home souvenirs of their holiday to remind them of happy, carefree days. In the past, each resort tended to have its own distinctive mementoes, but this is no longer so; souvenirs to be bought in one place are very much like those in another, and most of them are made far from the place where they are sold. The Channel Islands had their distinctive souvenirs like everywhere else. In Jersey and Guernsey replicas of the local milkcans were popular. In the former island could be bought cabbage walking-sticks, made from the stalks of the giant Jersey cabbages, about which there is a song entitled "It's Here We Grow the Cabbages Ten Feet High"; there was also china decorated with local views. Eau-de-Cologne, of which there were a number of local brands, was popular with the ladies, as was the beautiful blue stone found in Sark, which was mounted as jewellery. Unfortunately, Sark stone is no longer available in commercial quantities. Milkcans are still popular, and Jersey cabbage walking-sticks are having a limited revival. Eau-de-Cologne is still manufactured, but is not as popular as formerly. The traditional woollen knitted garments known as jerseys and guernseys (see Chapter XII) have a ready sale, as does the pottery manufactured in the islands. In Sark miniature lobster pots and baskets are still made by the old fishermen in the winter and sold to visitors as souvenirs. Needless to say, the vast majority of visitors avail themselves of the concessions allowed them by H.M. Customs!

XII

INDUSTRIES

Apart from the keeping of cattle and the raising of crops, fishing is the oldest industry in the Channel Islands. In medieval times fishing, particularly for conger and mackerel, was an important industry. There were special places called *éperqueries* for the drying of the fish. The place-name L'Eperquerie occurring in the north of Sark preserves the memory of those early days. Fishing is still carried on commercially, although possibly more so around Guernsey than Jersey. Lobsters yield high prices, but unfortunately the picturesque old-time lobster pots made of willow are giving way to ugly contraptions made largely of wire netting.

In view of the islanders' immemorial connection with the sea, it is not surprising that they were among the first from western Europe to take part in the cod fishing off the east coast of North America. The earliest reference to the Channel Islands' connection with this type of fishing occurs in 1582, and from then until the latter years of the nineteenth century it was an important industry which resulted in a three-way trade. The fishing boats were fitted out in the islands and sailed to the fishing grounds; the fishing completed and the catches sold to Catholic countries for fast days—Rio de Janeiro and Naples providing ready markets—they eventually headed for home with various cargoes which were either sold on the way or brought back to the islands. This routine was repeated year after year to the financial advantage of the participants—some of them built themselves new houses which were dubbed 'cod houses'—and to the islands.

In 1766 a young Jerseyman Charles Robin (1743–1824) established himself as a fish merchant in Gaspé in the Gulf of the St. Lawrence River in the Province of Quebec, Canada. It is interesting to note that after more than 200 years the firm which Robin founded still survives, although now known as Robin, Jones &

Walter and Charles Penney, makers of Guernsey milkcans
Fish Market, Guernsey, showing spider crabs

Whitman. In the early days there were rival Jersey firms, such as Hammond Dumaresq & Co. and Nicholas Fiott & Co.

Robin was not an isolated example of a Jerseyman establishing himself on the Gaspé coast, for many Jersey families went to live there, and as the years went by so little colonies were established and flourished in spite of being resented by their French neighbours. Sadly, with World War I and the decline of the fishery, these colonies have dwindled and the families of Jersey origin have been assimilated with the remainder of the population, who are principally of French descent. A few elderly islanders remain to recall the old days, but regretfully the time will arrive when stories of the cod-fishing industry and the considerable part it played in Jersey's way of life will no longer be a memory but will have become part of history.

Another aspect of fishing, this time particularly relating to Jersey, was the oyster fishery carried on from that island. In 1797 important oyster banks were discovered between Jersey and France, a few miles north-west of the French-owned Island of Chausey. After their discovery the banks were exploited by Jersey fishermen, until in 1810 a regular fishery was established to supply the chartered companies of Kent and Sussex. For fifteen years the fishery prospered. It was based on Gorey Harbour, with subsidiary harbours at Bouley Bay, La Rocque and Rozel. Between 200 and 300 fishing smacks were engaged in the trade, manned by some 2,000 seamen. Inglis wrote in 1834: "the spectacle (at Gorey) is not only animated, but beautiful, when on a fine spring afternoon, the fleet of fishing boats with full sails and bent masts is seen under the influence of a gentle breeze, making for their general rendezvous". The season lasted from late autumn until June, the greatest activity being between February and May. In addition to sailors, the industry gave employment to about 1,000 people, mainly women and boys, from the east side of the island. Again to quote Inglis: "The oysters after being brought to Gorey, are sorted; the large, are sent to St. Helier for sale— while the smaller are set apart for the English market; and it is from the Gorey fishery, that the Colchester oyster market is chiefly supplied." It may be gathered from this that the natives of Colchester were sometimes immigrants from Jersey.

In 1838 occurred the 'Battle of the Oyster Shells' resulting from an Act of the States of that year concerning the conduct of the

St. Sampson's Harbour, Guernsey
Island of Lihou from L'Erée Headland, Guernsey

Gorey oyster fishery and the laying down of new oyster beds at Grouville. The fishermen defied the prohibition against dredging in these new beds, and the Constable of St. Martin endeavoured to enforce the law, but without avail. The military were called out and fired on the defiant fishermen, who immediately submitted to the inevitable. The principal offenders were arrested, but were lightly dealt with. Unfortunately the Lieutenant-Governor, Major-General Archibald Campbell, who had gone to Gorey to supervise the operation, caught a chill from which he subsequently died.

The industry prospered until 1835 when hostile French action resulted in a restricted area of the oyster banks being available to the Jersey-based fishermen, which caused an immediate halving of the quantity of oysters usually obtained. However, the fishery continued, and in 1857 it reached its peak when some 179,690 tubs worth £37,248 were dredged.

It is hard to realize that there was a time when Jersey almanacs listed a number of oyster rooms all supplied with local oysters. For example, *The British Press and Jersey Times Royal Almanac for the year 1872* contains an advertisement inserted by J. Trenchard of the 'Royal George', 20 Halkett Street, St. Helier, which proclaims that his is a "Noted House for Oysters and Stout" and that he receives "Fresh Oysters daily during the Season". It may be added that there was a time when half a dozen oysters, brown bread and butter and a glass of stout could be had in Jersey for a shilling. And there was also a time when one guide-book was able to state that "Oysters will fetch but twopence per dozen, and still be the finest in the world!" Alas, this once thriving fishery was dead by the early 1870s, but the committee set up under Article 21 of the Law of 1882 lingered on as a standing joke until it was finally put out of its misery in 1937. A small oyster fishery was established in Guernsey in 1820 and lasted for a number of years.

Channel Islanders were very successful privateers. Many people confuse a privateer with a pirate. The essential difference between the two was that the former acted within the law under the authority of Letters of Marque (examples exist in both Jersey and Guernsey) and confined himself to attacking enemy shipping, while the latter operated on his own account attacking all shipping indiscriminately, even that of his own country. Privateering was abolished in 1856 by Article I of the Treaty of Paris. The eighteenth century and the first fifteen years of the nineteenth century saw Channel Islanders very substantially and successfully involved in privateering, some of them making fortunes as a result.

There is little doubt that Jersey, Guernsey and Alderney were deeply involved in smuggling during the eighteenth century. This illicit traffic took the form of the shipping of vast quantities of brandy, gin, rum, tea, tobacco and other dutiable goods into the United Kingdom through a network of agents and contacts. This unlawful but highly profitable industry was finally stopped by legislation at the beginning of the nineteenth century. A leading Guernsey firm involved in the traffic was Carteret Priaulx and Co.

Shipbuilding was carried on in Jersey and Guernsey, and there is little doubt that from the earliest times Channel Islanders built small fishing boats for use in local waters. The first mention of a boat being built in Jersey occurs in 1468 and the second not until 1789. The first permanent yard appears to have been that of George Deslandes, established in 1821. The industry prospered and some twenty-six shipyards are known to have existed at one time or another. By modern standards the ships built were very small, the vast majority being considerably below 1,000 tons. The ship *Rescue* (1187 tons) launched in 1862 is believed to have been the largest ever built in Jersey; the largest built in Guernsey was the ship *Golden Spur* (656 tons), launched in 1864. The industry had declined in Jersey by 1880 and was almost non-existent by 1890. The subsidiary trades of blockmaking, mast and oarmaking, ropemaking, sailmaking and ship and anchor-smithing were also carried on in the island. The first steamer built in Jersey was the S.S. *Don*, launched in 1851; the first, if not the only one, built in Guernsey was the S.S. *Commerce*, launched in 1874. The Guernsey industry was similar to that of Jersey, lasted from 1815 until 1895 and brought with it the same allied trades as in the sister island.

Channel Islands' sea captains—no doubt like their opposite numbers elsewhere—liked to possess pictures of the ships they commanded. Hundreds of pictures of ships owned in the islands were painted, and happily many of them are still in local ownership. There are two categories of these 'ship pictures'. First, those painted individually, which are in many cases workmanlike and pleasing examples of marine art; secondly, water-colours in which the vessels concerned are depicted in the Bay of Naples, with Vesuvius well in evidence. Backgrounds were prepared in advance; when a ship arrived at Naples the captain was asked if he would like a picture of his vessel, and if he wanted one it was then painted on one of the ready-made landscapes. A well-known Jersey marine artist P. J. Ouless (1817–85) was the grandson of Philip Joseph Oulez, a Frenchman, and Elizabeth Noel, a Jersey-woman, who were married in St. Andrew's Church, Guernsey, in 1787. A number of his works are preserved in the islands.

Two of the cargoes brought back to the islands in ships return-ing from the Newfoundland codfisheries were leather and mahogany, which provided the raw materials for the local boot and shoemaking and furniture industries. In 1850 between 14,000 and 15,000 pairs of shoes and 1,000 pairs of boots were exported from Jersey. A directory of 1872 lists no fewer than fifty-one boot and shoemakers, both individuals and firms, carrying on business in that island. Among their products were the seaboots worn by sailors and fishermen.

A large amount of good quality mahogany furniture of every description was made in Jersey and Guernsey during the eighteenth and nineteenth centuries; a leading maker in the latter island was a Mr. Guille. Unfortunately, much of it has succumbed to changes of fashion, and much of that which has survived has been bought by dealers from outside the islands. The island-made furniture generally followed conventional designs, and only experts are able to distinguish it from similar furniture made in the United Kingdom.

In passing it should be mentioned that there are surviving a large number of longcase clocks bearing on their dials the names of Channel Islands' 'clockmakers'. The oldest known example of a Jersey clock is in the style of the 1690s and bears the name of Henri de la Feuille, watchmaker, of St. Helier. It is highly doubt-ful whether these clocks were actually made in the islands. It is almost certain that the mechanisms were imported and assembled locally and that the cases were made in the islands.

Silver plate, both ecclesiastical and domestic, has existed in the Channel Islands throughout the centuries; some of this silver has been imported, but a great deal has been manufactured by local craftsmen. Pre-Reformation ecclesiastical plate is rare, only part of a chalice surviving in Jersey and one chalice and the Guille Cruet or Ampulla surviving in Guernsey. Ancient domestic silver is also rare and, like ecclesiastical silver, has suffered from the vicissitudes of history. No doubt a great deal of both kinds has been melted down, a fate suffered by a number of church vessels in Guernsey as late as the nineteenth century. Although until recently little interest was taken by dealers in Channel Islands' silver because not very much was known about it and it was never hallmarked (although makers' initials frequently appear), this is no longer the case, and a great deal of the silver has left the islands. Some of it has fetched remarkably high prices. Nevertheless, a great deal remains in private hands in the islands, and a fine collection is owned by the Société Jersiaise. Initialled spoons generally feature among privately held silver as it was the custom to give a silver spoon to a godchild and a set of teaspoons as a wedding gift. A wide variety of pieces were manufactured by the insular silversmiths—wine cups, porringers, christening bowls, shoebuckles, sword-hilts—the list is almost endless. Certain pieces, such as coffee-pots, tea-pots and forks, are rare; others, particularly spoons, are frequently to be met with. The Jersey christening bowls or marriage cups (the latter indicated by dual sets of initials following the French custom of the period) resembl shallow two-handled porringers and are unique to that island. Replicas of these bowls in various sizes are manufactured in England and are obtainable in Jersey, as are replicas of the two-handled Guernsey christening cups or porringers in Guernsey. The silversmiths of the Channel Islands were highly skilled, and some went to England and became very successful in their trade. For instance, the Guernseyman, Peter Perchard, Lord Mayor of London, was a successful silversmith and learnt the trade from his uncle, Matthew Perchard, who was a jeweller and goldsmith in Hatton Garden, London, and died in 1779, leaving what was for those days the vast sum of £30,000.

At one time Sark possessed silver mines, and their site may still be seen on Little Sark. The story of mining on the island started in 1834 when John Hunt located a vein of silver at Le Pot. A company was formed and a thirty-one years' lease was taken from the Lord of the Manor, Peter Le Pelley, which was later extended for a further eight years. Operations were carried out at Le Pot until 1836, when another vein was discovered and two existing galleries from the original shaft were extended into it. Subsequently, no less than four new shafts were sunk. Many thousands of ounces of silver and some lead were extracted from the mine, but, unfortunately, the venture proved a failure, and in 1852 Peter Carey Le Pelley, who was then Lord of the Manor, was obliged to sell the Lordship of Sark, owing to his financial involvement in the mine. It is interesting to note that a tea service, reputedly made of Sark silver, was put on display in St. Peter Port to encourage support for the mine, but unfortunately it is not known what happened to this unique service.

Most of the silver mined in Sark was exported to France, where the best price was to be obtained. None of it was used to make Channel Islands' plate, as by the time the mines were opened silver goods were no longer being manufactured locally.

Guernsey too, once had a silver mine, which was located at Mont Durand, St. Martin's, and exploited by the Blanchelande Mining Corporation during the 1840s. This enterprise was even less successful than the Sark mine; furthermore, the company found itself involved in litigation as its mining operations had resulted in the drying up of wells at St. Martin's.

At least as early as the beginning of the seventeenth century a large number of domestic utensils in use in the Channel Islands were made of pewter. It is unfortunate that there is little or no information regarding the native pewterers, even if they ever existed. There was, however, without any doubt, a definite Channel Islands' style of pewter, made in London. The museum in St. Helier contains specimens labelled with the following makers' names and dates: Jonas Durand (1692–1735), Hellier Perchard (1709), John de Ste. Croix (1729–30), E. Bonamy (1732–75), William de Jersey (1732–85) and Thomas Fassen (1783). In the reconstruction of an old Jersey kitchen in the same building may be seen other examples of pewter of local interest.

Presumably these pewterers were considered by the person responsible for the case and its labelling to be Channel Islanders, if not Jerseymen. Consultation of *Old Pewter Its Makers and Marks* by H. H. Cotterell provides additional information, but in no case does the author state that any of the above named were in fact from the Channel Islands. Jonas Durand may have been from one of the islands, and Cotterell lists two pewterers with the same two names. Perchard, judging by his combination of forename, spelt variously Hellary, Hellier and Hillier, and surname, was almost certainly a Jerseyman or of Jersey extraction. Hellier Perchard, who became Master of the Worshipful Company of Pewterers of London in 1740, used various marks. Cotterell also lists a Samuel Perchard, and it is likely that he was a relative of Hellier.

John de Ste. Croix (listed as de St. Croix) was a Jerseyman and actually incorporated the island's arms into one of his marks. On a flagon his mark usually is to be found on the inside of the lid. Two pewter flagons, each 10 inches high (one probably for water and the other for wine), one small flagon, one large pewter platter and two small pewter platters (probably alms dishes), all bearing either his mark, as previously mentioned, or his mark "I D S X", belong to St. Lawrence's Church, Jersey. Either the pewterer himself or someone with the same name presented a fine pewter platter to St. Helier's Church in the same island. It is inscribed on the rim "Don de Mr. Jean de Ste. Croix à la Paroisse de St. Hélier 1744."

Bonamy is not listed by Cotterell, and it is possible that he was a truly 'local' pewterer. Judging solely by name, de Jersey was a Guernseyman or of Guernsey extraction. In the Bulletin of the Société Jersiaise for 1936 there is printed a Certificate of Origin dated 20th July 1765, relating to the shipping by John de Ste. Croix, Senr., pewterer, Freeman of the City of London, of approximately 700 pounds of old pewter in the form of ingots to Mr. William de Jersey, pewterer, of Cannon Street, London. Thomas Fassen, whose surname appears in Cotterell as Fasson, was one of a number of pewterers of the same name. There is no evidence to indicate that any of them were connected with the Channel Islands. Finally, Cotterell lists a George Vibart. This name is similar to that of the Jersey surname Vibert and may in fact be a variation of it.

A Guernsey flagon is baluster-shaped, generally encircled by two broad bands around its swelled-out base and has a heart-shaped lid with twin acorn thumbpiece; a Jersey flagon is similar except that it lacks the two broad bands and has not such a swelled-out base. St. John's Church, Jersey, possesses two pewter flagons and four pewter platters, while St. Mary's Church, in the same island, has a large pewter platter. Two pewter flagons, each

10 inches high, one plain and one stamped, formerly used as
flagons for Communion, featured among the church plate of St.
Anne's, Alderney, before World War II. It would appear, on
enquiry, that these two flagons have been either lost or mislaid,
possibly as a result of the German Occupation. Official distinctive
Channel Islands' pewter un-lidded measures exist bearing the
Sovereign's crowned cypher and the initial J for Jersey. Examples
of Channel Islands' style pewter are also in private possession.

Just as Jersey and Guernsey are known for their cattle and their
agricultural and horticultural produce, so are they for the two
garments which bear their names—the jersey and the guernsey. A
jersey has been defined as a "close-fitting tunic, with short or long
sleeves, worn either as an outer tunic or as an under-shirt or
under-vest". The definition of a guernsey is similar. It should be
appreciated, however, that it was not only for these garments
that the islands were famous, they were also celebrated for other
knitted goods, especially stockings. The latter were esteemed
even by royalty and are known to have been worn by Queen
Mary I, Mary Queen of Scots (who wore a pair at her execution)
and Queen Elizabeth I.

The Channel Islands' knitting industry dates back certainly to
the sixteenth century, if not earlier. According to *The Shorter
Oxford English Dictionary* the name "jersey" was generally applied
to worsted as early as 1587. The raw material was principally
imported from England, Jersey being allowed 4,000 tods,
Guernsey 2,000, Alderney 400 and Sark 200. The industry reached
considerable proportions during the seventeenth and eighteenth
centuries. At one time some 6,000 pairs of stockings were made
in Jersey each week. The bulk of them was exported to France
and a few were sent to Spain; knitted waistcoats were exported
to England. The people were so taken up with knitting that in
1606 it was ordered by the Royal Court that knitting was not to
be carried on to the prejudice of the harvest and the gathering of
seaweed. Peter Heylyn writing in the seventeenth century had
this to say of Guernsey's knitting industry: "The principall com-
modity which they use to send abroad, are the works and labours
of the poorer sort, as Wast-cotes, Stockins, and other manu-
factures made of wool, wherein they are exceeding cunning."

The industry declined and by the early years of the nineteenth
century was dead, but it is pleasing to know that it has been

revived in both Jersey and Guernsey. In the former island jerseys are manufactured in a local knitting factory; in the latter the Women's Institutes played a large part in reviving the manufacture of the traditional guernseys and there are now several knitting businesses engaged in their production; the largest of these employs no fewer than 300 home knitters. Although the plain body and sleeves of the guernseys are worked by machine for commercial purposes, the more complicated parts are still worked by hand, and great care is taken to preserve the traditional pattern and quality. The design of the traditional guernsey varied from parish to parish in earlier times, but is now standardized. The various details and stitches were said to represent the ripples of sand, the floats of a fishing net and ladders of a ship's rigging. A special navy blue worsted wool, naturally oiled, was used, and the body of the garment was worked in plain knitting on seven or more double-ended stocking needles. Essential features of the garment are the garter stitch and rib welt with slit hemline, garter stitch panels on the body, diamond shaped under-arm gussets, grafted shoulder seams and triangular neck gussets. The Guernsey Federation of Women's Institutes issues its own pattern, and trophies are presented annually for the best work submitted, expert judges making sure that the traditional pattern is correct.

There is a great deal of granite in the Channel Islands. Among other rocks the conglomerate or pudding stone to be found in Jersey in the vicinity of Rozel is most striking. Granite has been quarried in all the islands, including Herm, Jethou and even the Ecréhous and Minquiers, and used in the construction of the islands' buildings. Its colour varies considerably, from pink right through to grey and blue. In course of time what was a purely local industry producing stone for local requirements, became, especially in the case of Guernsey, an important export industry, and in 1913 500,000 tons of granite were exported from the island, an all time record. The stone was shipped principally, if not entirely, from St. Sampson's Harbour. Granite from Herm was used fairly extensively in London, and the steps of the Duke of York's column in Waterloo Place are believed to have been made from it.

An important industry in the islands was cider-making, especially in Jersey, where at one time a large area of the island was covered with apple orchards and most farms had a cider trough and press. The industry existed from at least as early as the seventeenth century until about the end of the nineteenth century. In 1806 cider was one of Jersey's principal exports, and it continued to be so for a number of years. In 1832 no fewer than 564,768 gallons were exported. Sadly, like many other of Jersey's industries, cider-making declined, and by 1893, although cider was still being made for local consumption, it did not feature among a list of the island's industries. It is not surprising in a place so much engaged in the production of cider that a Jerseyman Francis Le Couteur (1744–1808) was an expert on the subject and wrote a book about it which was recognized as a standard work and adopted as such by the British Board of Agriculture, forerunner of the Ministry of Agriculture.

Many other smaller industries have been carried on in the islands at different times, of which perhaps the most important was brickmaking.

With all their different industries it is not to be wondered at that Jersey and Guernsey each possesses a Chamber of Commerce founded respectively in 1768 and 1808.

XIII

TRANSPORT

Until the nineteenth century the roads throughout the Channel Islands were generally narrow, often winding and always un-metalled. In winter they were muddy and in summer they were dusty; at all times they were scarred with ruts made by the wheels of the farm carts, which were virtually the only vehicular traffic using them. The old roads of Jersey were of various widths, the widest being 22 feet and the narrowest 3 feet 8 inches; in Guernsey they were generally the width of a cart, with lay-bys to allow vehicles to pass each other.

Until the Reformation the parish churches in Jersey not only possessed the *Franchise de l'Eglise* or right of sanctuary in accordance with Norman Law, but, in addition, from each church there was a *perquage* or sanctuary road leading to the sea, although not always by the shortest route. These special roads were used by those who had sought refuge in the churches and wished to leave the island. At the Reformation the right of sanctuary was abolished and the *perquages* became Crown property. It is thought that the last occasion when a *perquage* was used for its intended purpose was that of Trinity in 1558. By Letters Patent dated 30th May 1663, King Charles II made a grant of all the *perquages* and waste lands in Jersey to Sir Edward de Carteret, son of Sir Philip de Carteret, in recognition of the family's loyalty to him during the Civil War. The *perquages* were sold off piecemeal and eventually ceased to exist as roads, with the exception of about a half a mile of the St. Lawrence Perquage and the St. Brelade Perquage, which latter merely consists of a flight of stone steps descending from the churchyard of the parish church to the beach below.

Prior to the Reformation numerous wayside crosses were to be found in the islands, as is evidenced by existing place-names which incorporate the word 'cross', such as Hautes

Croix, St. John, and Croix au Maître, St. Martin, both in Jersey.

Until early in the nineteenth century the roads in the Channel Islands were those which had existed since time immemorial, and few, if any, new ones were ever built. However, when Sir George Don was lieutenant-governor of Jersey and Sir John Doyle lieutenant-governor of Guernsey, a number of roads were constructed in both islands for military purposes. It is these roads, together with a few others dating from the nineteenth century, which form the basis of the existing network of main roads. During the present century a few additional roads have been built, such as Val des Terres in Guernsey and La Route du Nord in Jersey. The latter is interesting for the reason that the greater part of it was built during the Occupation with a view to depriving the Germans of local labour which they might otherwise have used. Victoria Avenue, Jersey, originally opened in 1897 has been reconstructed so as to provide a dual carriageway. The method of surfacing roads known as macadamization after its inventor J. L. McAdam (1756–1836) was first used in England between 1810 and 1816, and it is surprising to discover that it was used in the western parishes of Jersey as early as 1824.

Despite the small area of the islands, they contain many hundreds of miles of roads, most of which are well maintained. The pressure on them in Jersey and Guernsey is tremendous in view of the large number of vehicles in circulation, especially in summer. Traffic regulations are stringent, and an islandwide speed limit of 40 miles per hour obtains in Jersey and one of 35 miles per hour in Guernsey. In Jersey the vehicle registration numbers are preceded by the letter J; this is not so in Guernsey where only the number appears.

Various types of agricultural carts were the only vehicles using the roads until the eighteenth century. Examples of old Jersey and Guernsey carts may be seen respectively in the Agricultural Museum at La Hougue Bie and in the Guernsey Folk Museum at Saumarez Park. It is believed that Sir John Dumaresq had the first carriage in Jersey in 1795 and that Lieutenant-Colonel Irving, the lieutenant-governor of Guernsey (1770–84), was the first person to have one in that island. It is, however, known that the first omnibus service in Jersey was opened by Richard Monck in 1788. It operated on Saturdays between 'The Swan', St. Aubin, and 'The Bunch of Grapes', Water Lane (now Wellington Road), on the outskirts of St. Helier. This is an early date for a bus service in the British Isles, and it has been pointed out that it was to be some twenty years before George Shillibeer started his omnibus service between the Bank and the 'Yorkshire Stingo' in London. Horse buses are known to have been in operation between St. Peter Port and St. Sampson as early as 1837. The first cabs in St. Helier were introduced in the 1850s. The first 'horseless carriage' made its appearance in Jersey in 1899, the owner being Peter Falla, a well-known local solicitor.

Bus services developed in both Jersey and Guernsey as did the tours operated by horse-drawn excursion cars, the forerunners of the motor char-à-bancs and motor coaches. Today there is only one bus company in Jersey, the Jersey Motor Transport Company Ltd., known for brevity as the 'J.M.T.', the livery of whose buses is blue and cream. A number of the company's old buses are preserved as vintage vehicles in the United Kingdom. In Guernsey there are two principal bus companies, The Guernsey Railway Company Ltd., and its associate company, Guernsey Motors Ltd. The colours of the former (adopted in 1935) are green body with a cream flare and of the latter maroon body with a cream flare. Jersey has had double-decker buses since 1931, but Guernsey has none.

Shipping has of necessity always provided the Channel Islands with their essential link with the outside world. The hazards of the sea have, however, always been and still are very real. One has only to see the rocks around the coasts of the islands to appreciate how dangerous they would be to shipping were it not for the skill of sea captains coupled with modern navigational aids. The group of rocks off the north coast of Jersey known as The Paternosters or Pierres de Lecq are said to have come by the former name because sailors were accustomed to recite the Lord's Prayer (Paternoster) whenever they passed them and this as a consequence of a shipwreck which occurred there in the sixteenth century and resulted in a number of children being drowned. The Casquets (see Chapter II) lying to the west of Alderney are a dangerous reef of rocks and have been the cause of many a ship being lost. As recently as 1899 the S.S. *Stella*, which was owned by the London and South Western Railway Company, while on a voyage from

Southampton to Guernsey struck the reef in fog and sank with the loss of 105 lives.

From the days when the islands were part of Normandy there was always sea traffic between the two, and, not surprisingly, the first lighthouse in the group was situated on the Ecréhous. The islands also had sea communications with France and England from early times. Southampton was the principal English port for Channel Islands' trade for many centuries.

Although there had always been constant sea communications between the islands and the outside world, there were no regular services in the modern sense until the introduction of the first Post Office sailing packets in 1794. The first of these vessels, the cutter *Earl of Chesterfield*, arrived in Jersey from Weymouth with the first mail on 18th February of that year; the other vessel on the service was the cutter *Rover*; a third packet, the *General Doyle*, joined the service in 1807. The Post Office packets were in competition with privately owned and operated vessels, which were ultimately to supersede them. The introduction of steamships marked another stage in the development of sea communications. The first steamer to visit Jersey was the *Medina*, which arrived at St. Helier on 11th June 1823. A new era dawned in 1845, when the contract for carrying the mails was given to the South Western Steam Packet Company, which was financed by the London and South Western Railway Company. This marked the beginning of the railway steamers, which have ever since provided the passenger services between the islands and the United Kingdom. A long succession of vessels have been employed, many of which have earned the affection of the travelling public. The *Caesarea* and *Sarnia*, now operating the service from Weymouth, are not the first vessels to bear those names. The first *Caesarea* was built in 1867 and saw seventeen years service, before being wrecked in fog; the second was built in 1910 and saw service until 1923, when she struck the Oyster Rock and sank outside St. Helier's Harbour; the third (the present vessel) came into service in 1960. The first *Sarnia* came into service in 1911; she was used as an armed boarding vessel in World War I and was sunk in 1918; the second (the present vessel) came into service in 1961.

The principal routes from the United Kingdom to the Channel Islands have always been between Weymouth or Southampton (now only Weymouth) and Guernsey and Jersey. Regular passenger services have been carried on between the islands and Carteret, Granville and St. Malo at different periods from the nineteenth century until the present day.

Of all forms of transport, the one which seems to have captured the lasting affection and interest of the travelling public is the railway. It should be noted, however, before any misunderstanding can arise, that this applies strictly to the steam railway, and particularly to the steam railway before the hand of modernization was laid so heavily upon it. The sight of a splendid steam engine with its paintwork gleaming and its brasswork shining, drawing an equally well-kept train, is among the treasured memories of those who have been privileged to see it.

The Channel Islands did not escape the great railway era, despite the fact that, except in Alderney, none remains to prove that railways once existed in those remote parts of the British Isles.

In both the principal islands the first mention of a railway appears in the newspapers of 1845, but nothing resulted, although a small temporary railway was used by the contractors building St. Catherine's Breakwater (1847–55) in Jersey, until 28th September 1870, when the Jersey Railway Co. Ltd., opened its line from St. Helier to St. Aubin. The total length of the line was about 3¾ miles. Initially, in addition to the termini at St. Helier and St. Aubin, there were three stations. The railway hotel at St. Aubin (now St. Brelade's Parish Hall) was opened in 1871. A number of additional stations were subsequently opened along the length of the original St. Helier – St. Aubin section of the line. An extension to La Moye Quarries was opened in 1884. The company went bankrupt, and eventually the whole of the railway from St. Helier to La Moye came into the ownership of the Jersey Railways Company Ltd., an English company, which itself went into voluntary liquidation in 1895. The following year the railway was taken over by Jersey Railways and Tramways Ltd., of which William Henry Venables Vernon (1852–1934), was chairman, as he was of the Guernsey Railway Company Ltd. until he became Bailiff of Jersey in 1899. The line was extended to Corbière in 1899. In 1923 a Sentinel–Cammell railcar was introduced to be followed by a further one the next year. Over a million passengers were carried by the company in both the years

1924 and 1925, but thereafter the numbers declined every year, as did the company's financial position. The causes of the trouble were the competition from buses and coaches and the increase in the number of private cars. The closure of the railway seemed inevitable, but what made it a certainty was the fire which occurred at St. Aubin's Station on the morning of 18th October 1936 and destroyed most of the company's rolling stock in store there for the winter. That was the end of the railway, and the last train to run on the 30th September, at the close of the summer season, proved to be the last ever to run on the line.

A number of the old stations survive, including the terminus at St. Helier, now partly occupied by the States' Tourism Department and Information Bureau, and the station at Corbière, now a house and café.

In passing, it is worth mentioning that in 1923 the company started to operate its own bus services to connect with its railway services and five years later took over the Jersey Motor Transport Co. Ltd. (referred to earlier), which had also been established in 1923.

The Jersey Eastern Railway operated a line from Snow Hill, St. Helier, to Gorey Harbour, a distance of about 6¼ miles. The line was opened in 1873 and extended to Gorey Harbour in 1891. Sentinel-Cammell railcars were introduced in 1927. The company, unable to withstand competition from road transport, ceased to operate in 1929. It is of interest to note that at one time Major Gilbert More, father of Kenneth More the actor, was manager of the company, which is how it was that his son came to attend Victoria College.

In 1879 the Guernsey Steam Tramway Co. Ltd. opened a tramway between the harbours of St. Peter Port and St. Sampson, a distance of just under 3 miles. In 1891 the line was electrified and was one of the first electric railways in the British Isles to have an overhead system. The tramway company bought out the Guernsey Omnibus Company in 1895. During World War I women were employed both as conductors and tram drivers. As with the railways in Jersey, the running of the tramway became uneconomical, and in 1934 it was closed.

Alderney's railway was opened in 1847 and is now used solely in connection with foreshoring along the breakwater at Braye. This is an endless operation as the foreshore is constantly being

Royal Connaught Square, Alderney (the smaller tree was planted by the present Queen)

Carriages at top of Harbour Hill, Sark, awaiting arrival of visitors

swept away owing to the considerable seas which build up there during strong easterly and north-easterly gales.

The first reference to flying in the Channel Islands would appear to be an entry in *La Gazette de l'Ile de Jersey* of Saturday 5th June 1790, which announced that Mr. Granger, M.A., of Angers University, a master at St. Mannelier's School in that island, would send up a balloon 90 feet in circumference on the following Saturday, subject to the weather being fine. In the issue of the same newspaper of 12th June it was announced that the event would take place at 6 p.m. that day in the courtyard of the hospital. On this occasion it was mentioned that the balloon was to be 36 feet in height and 104 feet in circumference. On 19th June it was announced that the same day at 5 p.m. Mr. Granger would send up a very large balloon from the Mont de la Ville. The balloon duly rose and remained airborne for 45 minutes and then dropped into the sea. The two events were financed by subscription, but from the *Gazette* of 3rd July it appears that Mr. Granger was somewhat out of pocket. It should be added that the first airmail letter to Jersey was carried by balloon from Paris in 1870.

The next landmark in Jersey aviation history occurred in 1912, when four seaplanes taking part in an air race from St. Malo to the island and back landed in St. Aubin's Bay, where they were refuelled.

Guernsey entered the aviation scene when a French seaplane station was established there during World War I. A flying-boat service (believed to have been the first in the British Empire) between Southampton and St. Peter Port was started in 1923, but it did not prove successful and was discontinued. Nevertheless, flying had come to stay, and the Channel Islands' routes were gradually improved.

Jersey Airways Ltd. was formed on 9th December 1933, and some nine days later the first aircraft took off from the beach at West Park, St. Helier, bound for Portsmouth. Permission for the beach to be used as a landing strip was given by the Receiver-General. During the company's first year of operation 20,000 passengers were carried. Originally the service was confined to Jersey-Portsmouth, but in January, 1934, an alternative Jersey-London service was started, to be followed in March of the same year by a Jersey-Southampton service. In June a bi-weekly

The Shell Beach, Herm, looking north

Jersey–Paris service was commenced, but ran into difficulty owing to colorado beetle control and had to be suspended in September. The number of passengers travelling by air to the islands steadily increased—24,717 were carried in 1935 and more than 30,000 the following year. Nowadays hundreds of thousands of passengers travel annually by air to and from the islands.

The first airport in the Channel Islands was opened in Alderney in 1935, the States of Jersey Airport at St. Peter was opened in 1937 and the States of Guernsey Airport at La Villiaze, Forest, in 1939. The three airports are maintained to the highest standards and have undergone many improvements since they were first established. There is also a helicopter landing pad on the Minquiers.

XIV

CUSTOMS AND CEREMONIES

The Channel Islands were once rich in customs and ceremonies, some of which were of ancient origin, dating back in a few instances at least to pre-Christian times. Unfortunately, many of these survivals have died out, some as the result of changing times, but others because of a regrettable lack of interest.

In Jersey public holidays and bank holidays are governed by the Public Holidays and Bank Holidays (Jersey) Act 1952 and Acts made thereunder. This legislation prescribes that New Year's Day shall be a public holiday and that should this day fall on a Sunday the 2nd January shall be a public holiday instead. In Guernsey New Year's Day is also a public holiday when the Bailiff gives a reception in his chambers, as do the Constables of St. Peter Port in their office.

On 6th January the anniversary of the Battle of Jersey used to be celebrated in that island, but this is no longer the case.

The Christmas Chief Pleas of the Royal Court of Guernsey are held on the Monday after St. Maurus' Day, 15th January. Jonathan Duncan wrote of the Chief Pleas in 1841:

The persons convened at the present meetings of the chief pleas are the bailiff, the governor, the jurats, the crown officers, the tenants *in capite* or lords of fiefs, the bordiers, the constables of the various parishes, and the advocates. Of these the bailiff and jurats now alone exercise the power of making ordinances. The governor, for whom the sheriff is always sent by the court, but who does not attend, has a deliberative voice, but no vote. The king's attorney or solicitor-general submits the matters to be taken into consideration. The constables and advocates attend merely, it is supposed, that they may be informed of such changes as may be made in the laws.

The representatives of the spiritual and temporal lords, though pompously proclaimed at every sitting, as, for instance, the bishop of Winchester (who stands in the place of the abbot of Coutances), the abbot of Mount St. Michael, the abbot of Blanchelande, the abbot of St. Geoffrey's cross, the lord of Anneville, of Saumarez and others, who also sat, as originally in England, by virtue of their tenures,—these, as well as the *bordiers*, one of whom rejoices in the singular cognomen of Fantôme, or Phantom, (which would admirably apply to the whole body of lords and bordiers), attend apparently for no earthly purpose whatever, unless it be for affording—like the *ghosts* or *phantoms* of things that once were—a perpetual memorial of the constitution of the ancient *states*, now merged into the court of chief pleas. . . .

Today the Court of Chief Pleas consists of the bailiff and the jurats and is attended by the law officers of the Crown, the greffier, prévôt and sergeant, the advocates, the tenants of fiefs owing suit of court and a constable from each parish. From the point of view of ceremony, there is little to distinguish a sitting of the Court of Chief Pleas from an ordinary sitting of the court, except for the calling of the roll, when each of the persons named above indicates his presence, the tenants at the Bar and the remainder standing in their respective places.

In Jersey by a law of 1928 it is permissible to cut seaweed (see Chapter X) from sunrise on Monday until sunset on Saturday from 1st February until 30th April, both dates inclusive. In Guernsey the cutting of seaweed is permitted between 15th July and 15th April.

The Quarter Days in Jersey are the same as in England and were fixed by the Chief Pleas of the Court of Heritage on 25th April 1757

In Jersey on Quarter Days the contents of Le Tronc were distributed. A collection of letters by an anonymous writer published in 1828 had this to say of Le Tronc:

A long iron box, called Le Tronc, is perpendicularly inserted in the wall on the outside of every church, to receive the alms of the charitable for the poor, and a tablet with this sentence above it: "Celui qui a pitié du pauvre preste à L'Eternal, qui lui rendra son bienfait" (He that hath pity upon the poor lendeth unto the Lord, and that which he hath given will He pay him again). Collections are also made every Sunday at the church doors; which, with the contents of the troncs, are distributed every quarter by the Minister, Principaux, Constable, and other officers, among the poor of the parish, in ailment or vestments as their wants require.

There were a number of Channel Islands' customs relating to Shrove Tuesday, Lent, Easter and Whitsun.

On Shrove Tuesday it was the custom to eat pancakes as it still is. In Jersey was observed on that day, as well as on Easter Monday and other holidays, a very unpleasant custom called La Jouôte, taking the form of a cockshy. Stones and sticks were thrown at the unfortunate cocks and rabbits which were used as targets, and those who killed one had it for a prize. Naturally only the skinniest birds and rabbits were donated for the purpose. Happily, this unpleasant custom was ended by legislation in 1896.

On the first Sunday in Lent it was the custom in Jersey, Guernsey and Alderney for the young people of each district to assemble at a given spot where a bonfire was lit around which they danced. Wisps of straw were lit and bandied about. In Alderney one of the places where the custom was observed was at La Pointe de Clonque. The day was known as La Dimanche des Brandons.

Good Friday was marked in both Jersey and Guernsey by a picnic at the seaside, the principal fare being limpets gathered and cooked on the spot, *gâche à fouée* (in Jersey), or bread cake (in Guernsey) with plenty of butter, possibly washed down with cider or beer. Hot cross buns were not introduced until some time in the nineteenth century. In Jersey one was awakened between 6 and 7 a.m. on a Good Friday by a small boy out in the street carrying a basket of hot cross buns with a cloth over it and crying:

> Hot cross buns!
> Hot cross buns!
>
> One a penny poker;
> Two a penny tongs.
>
> You've got the money;
> I've got none.
> Buy my buns
> And I'll have some.
> One-a-penny;
> Two-a-penny,
> Hot cross buns!
> Hot cross buns!
> All hot! All hot!

In Sark on Good Friday there was observed an unusual custom of which a former Vicar of the island has left the following description, published in 1875:

In Sark, on Good Friday, it is the custom for boys to go and sail small boats on the ponds or pools by the sea-shore; and these boats are made a good while beforehand, or treasured up of long standing; this custom they never fail to keep up. Numbers of these same boys also go in the afternoon to the Eperquerie drill-ground, to play a game which they call rounders. It is played with a ball and a stick, and somewhat resembles cricket.

Toy boats are still sailed on Beauregard Pond on Good Friday mornings, although the practice is gradually dying out.

The traditional fare for the midday meal on Easter Sunday in the country in Guernsey and in Sark was eggs and bacon. Today this custom continues in Sark, where some native islanders still eat either fish, bacon and eggs or just eggs for their midday meal on that day (for Jersey's Easter dishes see Chapter IX).

In Jersey there were a number of customs associated with Easter Monday. The day is a public holiday as it is in the other islands. William Plees observed in his book on the island, published in 1817: "Like the lower classes in England, many inhabitants, even some of a rather higher order, assemble in jovial parties on Easter Monday. The most general place or rendezvous is near the old castle [Gorey Castle]." Another writer observed in 1834: "Easter is not only a season for feasting, but for new dresses; and a great fair which is then held at Gorey, affords an opportunity of displaying them." Until about the mid nineteenth century it was the custom for many people from throughout the island, but more especially from the four eastern parishes, to make a pilgrimage to Gorey Castle on Easter Monday "this being the only day of the year that free admission was given to the public. From midday to nightfall, all roads led to the Castle, and everybody went on foot". This practice of visiting the castle appears to have been a survival of the pre-Reformation custom of making a pilgrimage on St. George's Day (23rd April) to St. George's Chapel, which stood within the castle's walls. In those days so many people took part that the authorities were alarmed lest the castle be overwhelmed and taken by the crowd and consequently the number of pilgrims was restricted.

On 1st April, All Fools' Day is observed by children in the islands. An April Fool is called in Jersey–French '*un paisson d'avri*' and in Guernsey–French '*aën fo d'avril*'.

In Jersey it was usual in time past on the first Sunday in May—Milk-a-Punch Sunday—for the young people, the girls dressed in white, to go out from the town of St. Helier into the neighbouring countryside, such as Vallée des Vaux (Ducks' Valley), to milk the cows, take the eggs from the hens and make milk punch. In fact, at one time there was a house in the valley called Milk Punch House. William Plees wrote in 1817: "During the month of May the environs of St. Helier's are, early every morning, crowded with the youth of both sexes, who in groups walk to different farm houses, for the purpose of drinking milk, warm from the cow." In Guernsey it was customary on 1st May for the young men and women from the poorer homes to get up at dawn and go into the country in parties, returning home with large bunches of flowers 'acquired' from cottage gardens. In Alderney Milk-a-Punch Sunday was also observed on the first Sunday in May and still is. There were also celebrations on the first three days of the month, when beribboned garlands were hung up where dancing was indulged in by the children and young people early in the day and by the grown-ups after the day's work was over. The dance called 'Mon beau Laurier' was the most popular on this occasion.

Liberation Day (9th May) is observed as a holiday in Jersey, Guernsey and Sark and holds a special place in the hearts of those islanders who lived through the German Occupation. In Sark a parade of decorated carriages and carts used to be held on that day, but the practice has been discontinued. Liberation Day is not celebrated in Alderney because the whole population was evacuated before the Occupation, and therefore there was no one to liberate when the Germans surrendered in 1945.

In Jersey a ceremonial sitting of the Assize of the Court of Heritage is held twice a year—generally on the first Thursday after 4th May and on the Thursday preceding 11th October. At one time these sittings lasted longer and were more colourful than they are today. The court comprises the bailiff and the twelve Jurats; the lieutenant-governor also attends. The law officers and the viscount are in attendance. The holders of certain of the principal manors attend to answer (the technical term is to make 'comparence') for them. Their names are read out by the Attorney General and each lord or lady of the manor stands up and answers "*garde*" (which in effect means "I am present") and then sits down. Should a lord of the manor fail to attend personally or be represented by an attorney on three consecutive occasions he forfeits his manor to the Crown. The advocates, all of whom have to be present, then rise in a body and renew their oath of advocate, after which the sitting ends. The halberdiers (who form a guard of honour for the court and the lieutenant-governor up the staircase and along the passage from the law library to the court room) are then inspected by the lieutenant-governor on the steps of the court house.

In the days when the insular militias existed the anniversary of Queen Victoria's birthday (24th May) was the occasion for holding a grand review in Jersey and Guernsey at which the local militias paraded at full strength and were inspected by the respective lieutenant-governors. In Jersey before the date of the review was changed to 24th May it was held on 29th May in honour of the Restoration of King Charles II in 1660. On review days the militiamen were very proud of themselves, more so than their military bearing, the fit of their uniforms and the sound made by their martial music entirely justified. In both islands the review finished with the firing of a *feu de joie*.

The 29th May is Oak Apple Day. In 1809 John Stead wrote of its celebration in Jersey as follows:

On the King's Warren [Gorey] it has been a custom for several Years, for many Gentlemen of the Island to assemble on the 29th of May and hold a Feast in Honour of the happy Restoration of Charles the 2nd, and the Overthrow of Fanaticism. At a Meeting of this Description, on the 29th of May, 1807 . . . his Excellency Lieutenant General Don, the present Deputy Governor attended.

This occasion was the last official celebration of Oak Apple Day in Jersey. However, the day was remembered by school children up to recent years. Any child not sporting an oak leaf on his or her clothing on that day was liable to be asked by fellow scholars whether he or she would have a "pinch or punch" as punishment for failing to observe the custom. The oak leaves were worn until noon, but if worn after then the wearer would likewise receive a pinch or punch.

The 23rd June is St. John's Eve, at which time a curious custom was observed, particularly in the Parish of St. John, Jersey; it was known as *faire braire les poëles* (to make the pans bray). Stead, again writing in 1809, referred to it thus:

In this Parish [St. John's], and indeed in most parts of the Island, a Custom prevails of which the Origin is unknown; on the Eve of St. John's Day, several Persons in different Parts of the several Parishes assemble their respective Neighbours, a large Brass Boiler, (in ordinary use as a Kitchen Utensil), is taken into the Yard and partly filled with Water, in which Spoons, drinking Utensils, Candlesticks, &c. of Metal, are immersed; a strong species of Rush is then attached to the Rim of the Boiler, to which other Rushes are tied; having been thoroughly wetted, Persons of both Sexes then lay hold of each Rush, and drawing their Hands quickly upwards and often repeating the Application, cause a Vibration of the Boiler and other Articles that produces a most dolorous and terrific Sound, which is encreased by the blowing of Cow's Horns: the Exercise forms altogether a discordant Noise, almost as loud as a Chinese Gong. This uncommon Amusement is continued for several Hours, 'till the Performers are weary and deafened with their Sport. It is called, *faire braire les Poëles*; the same Custom prevails in the neighbouring Province of Normandy.

William Plees wrote an account of the custom in 1817 together with a description of the events which followed it:

How extraordinary soever this recreation may be, it would be well if it ended in the innocent though discordant manner just described; but, unhappily, it has introduced another custom, which is of an injurious nature. After the sport is over, parties of men and boys go about the country, and from all the cows they can find take the milk, for sillabubs, puddings, &c, for the following day. They also make depredations in the gardens. This conclusive amusement is however now much restrained, and by magisterial vigilance will, probably, in a few years be entirely suppressed.

Plees also mentioned that: "At Midsummer the natives of Jersey and Guernsey . . . pay visits to their relations and friends in the sister island, and remain some time with them."

J. H. L'Amy wrote in 1927 of Midsummer's Day (or St. John's Day) as follows:

The customs formerly observed on Midsummer Day in Jersey are undoubtedly of Pagan origin although their significance is unknown.

One was for the fishermen of the district to circumnavigate a rock known as 'Le Cheval Guillaume' in St. John's Bay. It was also customary to light bonfires at various spots, and to indulge in Bacchanalian dances around them.

Inglis writing nearly a century earlier stated: "There is also a fair on St. John's Day, in the parish of St. John; and upon this occasion, more than any other, dancing is one of the amusements." This fair was abolished as a result of an Act of the States of 1797, which was passed following complaints of disorders at the fair. In Guernsey a Midsummer's Day fair was held at Castel in a field next to the parish church; similar fairs were held there at Easter and Michaelmas.

Until recent years horns were still blown in Jersey just before sunset on 24th June. It is said that this was done to remind people to pay the rental for their land, which in the case of farms and farmland is payable on that day. However, the custom has a far more ancient ring about it, and its true origin has been lost in the mists of antiquity.

One of the prerogatives of the ancient court of the Priory of St. Michael of the Vale in Guernsey was the triennial inspection of the king's highways throughout the island, which generally took place in the month of June. This inspection, known as La Chevauchée de St. Michel (Cavalcade of St. Michael) was without any doubt the most colourful and elaborate ceremony ever to have existed in the Channel Islands. The last time it was carried out (other than a revival in 1966 as part of the celebrations for the nine-hundredth anniversary of the Battle of Hastings) was on 31st May 1837. A full description of the cavalcade as it was held in the latter years of its existence appears in Sir Edgar MacCulloch's *Guernsey Folk Lore*, edited by Edith F. Carey and published in 1903, as follows:

27th April, 1813.—The Chevauchée of His Majesty is appointed to take place on Wednesday, the 9th of the following June, for the reparation of the quays and roads of the King, and it is ordered that it shall be published throughout the parishes of this island, and cried in the Market Place, so that no one can plead ignorance.

The 27th of May, 1813.—Before Thomas Falla, Esq., Seneschal of the Court and Jurisdiction of the Fief St. Michel, present, Messieurs James Ozanne, Nicholas Le Patourel, James Falla, Pierre Falla, Jean Mahy, Richard Ozanne, Nicholas Moullin, Daniel

Moullin, and Jean Le Pettevin (called Le Roux), vavassors of the said Court. The Court being to-day assembled to regulate the order to be pursued on Wednesday, the 9th of June proximo,—the day appointed by the Court for the Chevauchée of His Majesty to pass— has ordered that all the pions be dressed uniformly as follows, to wit: Black caps with a red ribbon behind. White shirts, with white cravats or neckerchiefs. Circular white waistcoats, with a red ribbon border. Long white breeches, tied with red ribbon round the knee. White stockings, and red rosettes on their wands.

And Messieurs les Prévôts of the Court are ordered to warn all those who are obliged to assist at the said Chevauchée to find themselves with their swords, their pions, and their horses, the aforesaid 9th of June at seven o'clock in the morning at the Court of St. Michael, according to ancient custom, in default of appearance to be subject to such penalties as it shall please the Court to award him. And also shall Monsieur Le Gouverneur be duly warned, and Thomas Falla, Esq. seneschal, and Messrs. Jean Mahy and Nicholas Moullin, vavassors, are nominated by the Court to form a committee so as to take the necessary measures to regulate the conformity of the said act concerning the dress of the pions.

(Signed) Jean Ozanne, Greffier.

On the above day, conformably to the said Act, all the pions, dressed in the afore-mentioned costume, met at seven o'clock in the morning at the Court of St. Michael, and there also were found the King's officers, vavassors, who had to serve there as esquires. The King's officers and the seneschal each had two pions on either side of his bridle rein, the vavassors were only entitled to one.

They began with a short inspection and a good breakfast on the emplacement east of the Vale Church. After breakfast, the members of the cortège, with their swords at their sides, got on their horses opposite the said Court of St. Michael, where the greffier of the said Court said the customary prayer, and the seneschal read the proclamation, and then they started. . . .

Whilst they are on their march, the five sheriffs carry by turns a white wand in the following order:—

The Sheriff of the Vale, from the Vale Church to the end of Grand Pont.

The King's Sheriff, from the end of Grand Pont, as far as the Forest.

The Sheriff of Grand Moûtier, from the Forest to the King's Mills.

The Sheriff of Petit Moûtier, from the King's Mills to the Douit des Landes in the Market Place, and the Sheriff of Rozel from the last mentioned place to the Vale.

During the procession the lance bearer carried a wand of eleven and a quarter feet long, and any obstacle this wand encountered, stones of walls, branches of trees, etc., had to be cleared away, and the proprietor of the obstacle was fined thirty sous, which went towards the expenses of the dinner. From time immemorial the privilege of the pions,—who were chosen for their good looks—was that of kissing every woman they met, whether gentle or simple, their only restriction being that only one pion was allowed to kiss the same lady, she had not to run the gauntlet of the gang. This privilege of course was invariably exercised!

At the entry of the Braye du Valle the seneschal freed the pions from their attendance on the bridle reins, and gave them authority to embrace any woman they might encounter, recommending good behaviour and the rejoining of their cavaliers at the Hougue-à-la-Perre.

The Chevauchée then went to Sohier, les Landes, la rue du Marais, la Grande Rue, la Mare Sansonnet, les Bordages, la Ronde Cheminée, and les Morets. Arriving at the Hougue-à-la-Perre the pions regained their respective stations on the side of their officers, leading the horses, and there, at ten o'clock, they were met by His Excellency Sir John Doyle, the Lieutenant-Governor and his staff, the horses of which were all decorated with blue ribbons, except those of the said Governor and of his family, who, out of compliment, carried red ribbons, matching those of the Chevauchée. The Bailiff, with his party and John Guille, Esq., also joined them at this spot, uniformly dressed in blue jackets, white trousers, and leghorn hats.

The whole cavalcade then moved on, the Governor and suite at the rear, preceded by the band of the town regiment, dressed as rustics, in long white jackets and large hats with their brims turned down, and followed by six dragoons to bring up the rear. Having passed between eleven and twelve o'clock through Glatney, Pollet, Carrefour, and High-street, they came to the Town Church, where they made the tour around a large round table which had been placed near the westerly door of the said church, which table was covered with a white cloth and supplied with biscuits, cheese, and wine, which had been provided by one of the 'sous-prévôts,' and the Sheriff and the King's Sergeant, on foot, offered each cavalier who passed the door food and drink.

During this interval the band played serenades and marches.

At noon they proceeded through Berthelot-street to the College fields, and, passing through the Grange, they reached the Gravée; here His Excellency took his leave. The cavalcade passed on by St. Martin's road to the ancient manor of Ville-au-Roi, one of the oldest habitations in the island. The entrance was tastefully decorated with arches of flowers and a crown in the centre, with flags flying, and, on one of the arches, 'Vive la Chevauchée.' Here, according to old manorial custom, the party was gratuitously regaled with milk. The procession then moved on by Les Câches to Jerbourg, with the exception of the pions, who proceeded to the village of the Forest, and there waited the return of the Court. Here they danced and amused themselves as before, and being rejoined by the cavalcade at the Bourg they moved on by Les Brulliots, and passing Torteval Church arrived at a house called the Château des Pezeries at Plein-mont, where a marquee was erected, and cold meats and wine were prepared for the gentlemen. The pions were seated on the grass in a circle which had been hollowed for them, in the shape of a round table, and they also had their repast. Here the procession halted till four o'clock, and by this time were joined by many carriages, filled with ladies and gentlemen, who, with a numerous party of all ranks, moved on by Rocquaine, Roque Poisson, below the Rouvets, Perelle, where a particular stone lies, which they are obliged to go round according to an old custom, from there by the Saint Saviour's Road to the Grands Moulins or King's Mills. On their arrival there they were rejoined by the pions, the mill was put in motion, and the miller came out with a plate in each hand, one containing flour of wheat, and the other of barley, which had been ground that instant by the mill. The miller then placed himself on a large stone, and the procession moved round him; this custom has prevailed from time immemorial. The procession then continued by St. George, La Haye du Puits, Saumarez, Le Camp du Roy, Les Salines, to the Clos du Valle, to the aforesaid Court of St. Michael, where they arrived about seven o'clock, and where they were again joined by the Lieutenant-Governor, the Bailiff, and some of the principal residents. The Court having been dismissed they all partook of a sumptuous dinner, at which Mr. Seneschal Falla presided. The pions were also handsomely entertained.

The custom which in Jersey most closely resembles that of the Cavalcade of St. Michael is the Visite Royale, an official visit by the Royal Court each year to two parishes (it follows that it takes six years to visit all twelve) carried out on two days, traditionally between Midsummer's Day and harvest time. The procedure has altered little since Charles Le Quesne wrote of it in 1856 thus:

I allude to a visitation or survey of the public roads by the body of the Court four times [now twice] a year. This takes place out of term. The Court on the day appointed meet usually near the parish church. They examine the parish books, produced by the constable, concerning the amount received for the roads, the persons who owe cartages or labour for the roads, and the manner in which the money is expended. The constable is then called upon to produce a jury of twelve good and impartial men, chosen from among his parishioners. The jury take an oath to lead the Court through the worst roads in the parish. These men are called les Voyeurs, because on the march, they see or discover the nuisances which may exist, the encroachments which may have been made, and the trees which, interfering with the free use of the road, should be removed. Formerly the procession was on horseback; now it is otherwise. The voyeurs, with the constable, take the lead; then follow the vicomte, with a staff, the bailiff and the jurats, accompanied by the attorney-general and the greffier. Whenever the voyeurs discover any nuisance or impediment in the road, or an unfortunate tree which has been guilty of an encroachment, they make a verbal report of the same to the Court, who immediately order the removal of the nuisance or the downfall of the tree. As all proprietors of land bordering on the public roads are bound to keep their hedges properly trimmed, and also to have the trees pruned in such a manner as not to overhang the road below a certain height, it is a rule that if the official staff of the vicomte, as he paces along the road, is arrested by an overhanging branch, a report is made to the Court, who, ascertaining that the report is correct, impose a fine on the owner of the land.

After the peregrination of the day is over, a dinner [nowadays a lunch] is provided by the Crown for the Court, and another for the voyeurs.

A great annual event in Jersey is the world famous Battle of Flowers, which was first held on 9th August 1902 to celebrate the coronation of King Edward VII. It was such a success that it was continued annually until World War I. 'The Battle' was revived in 1928 by private enterprise, the scene of the event being changed from Victoria Avenue, where it had previously been held, to Springfield Show Grounds. World War II put a stop to the event, but it was again revived in 1951 since when it has been held each year at Victoria Avenue. 'The Battle' is now held on the last Thursday in July and marks the culmination of the tourist season. Over the years exhibitors have acquired a great deal of skill in designing, constructing and decorating the floats and many of the exhibits, some of which are very large, attain a very high standard. Originally the flower most used in decorating the floats was the hydrangea, which grows in great profusion in the island, but nowadays a wide variety of flowers is used. The decorated arena stretches along Victoria Avenue from West Park to First Tower and is lined on either side with stands, benches and chairs. Part of the northern side is backed by the green slopes of Westmount and the whole of the southern side by the sea. Generally the weather is good for this popular event, and the arena is filled with thousands of spectators, programme sellers, ice-cream vendors, marshals, police, photographers and many more besides. The exhibits, divided into various classes, are interspersed with bands and during the course of the afternoon traverse the whole length of the arena several times. 'The Battle' used to bring the spectacle to a close, and during the short time it lasted the exhibits were stripped of their flowers, which were thrown at the crowd by the competitors and by the crowd back at the competitors and at each other. The actual 'Battle' has been discontinued for some years and the once familiar smell of squashed hydrangeas, which used to scent the air, is now a thing of the past. A few of the entries are preserved and are entered for the carnival procession at the St. Brelade's Fête, held on the Thursday following 'The Battle'. Guernsey also holds a Battle of Flowers each year at Saumarez Park.

In Alderney a week of festivities, known as Alderney Week, is held every year in August.

From September and throughout the winter friends and neighbours used to meet each evening at one another's houses to sit, knit and talk. These meetings were known as 'Les Veilles'. The first of such meetings was known as 'L'Assise de Veille' and was a particularly convivial and happy occasion. At 'Les Veilles' folk tales were told by the ancients and others as they sat by the fire on the Jonquière, which was a bench usually covered with dried bracken. Thus it was that by the dim light provided by the crasset lamps (they resembled pap boats in shape and gave a dim light) the old stories and legends were passed on from one generation to another.

The 5th November is celebrated as Guy Fawkes night as in other parts of the British Isles.

In Jersey at Christmas there is observed a custom relating to the ringing of church bells. The origin of this observance is not known, but is said to date from the French Occupation 1461–68. The custom is observed in the parishes of St. Mary, St.

Ouen and St. Peter. The bells are supposed to be rung continuously for thirty-six hours from noon on Christmas Eve until midnight on Christmas Day; in fact they are only rung intermittently and not at all when services are in progress.

The old and widely held belief that the cattle kneel down in their stalls at midnight on Christmas Eve in adoration of the Saviour is also held in the Channel Islands.

On New Year's Eve it was customary earlier this century for a crowd to gather in the Royal Square in Jersey to see the New Year in. Although the practice has been discontinued, nevertheless, there is no lack of celebration on that particular evening throughout the Channel Islands and at the first stroke of midnight a galaxy of glasses is raised to the New Year.

In the Channel Islands there were customs relating to those three important events in life, baptism, marriage and death. In Jersey silver christening cups and spoons were given to infants at their baptism (see Chapter XII). Cinnamon water was drunk at christening festivities.

In both Jersey and Guernsey it was once the custom on the evening of a marriage for the neighbours to fire a *feu de joie* outside the newly married couple's home as it was on the Sunday following the wedding for the couple to attend church 'to pay their regards'. Unfortunately marriages are not always happy, and in time past in Guernsey if it became known to their neighbours that a couple were always quarrelling Chevaucherie d'Ane (Donkey Music) was inflicted on them by the young men of the neighbourhood, who with two of their number mounted back to back on a donkey serenaded them with 'music' produced by striking pots and pans together and by the blowing of conch shells. This custom has been observed within living memory

An old custom which was observed in Sark as recently as 1959 was to send two persons to notify friends and relations of a person's death and to give them particulars of the funeral arrangements. These messengers were known as '*avertisseurs*'. The custom was formerly observed in Guernsey.

As in many other places, in Guernsey when a person who owned bees died they had to be 'told' of the death, and a black crêpe bow was attached to the hive.

Funerals in Jersey (and in the other islands) were more widely attended than in England, quite distant relatives being expected to

The west coast of Jethou
Razor-bills (left) and puffins on rocks at Burhou with Alderney in background

attend. Black crêpe hat-bands and gloves were provided by the undertaker for the mourners, who were almost exclusively male. At one time dues were exacted by each rector through whose parish the funeral passed and he met it at the parish boundary and accompanied it from its entry into the parish until its departure. A meal was provided for the mourners after the interment. On the Sunday following the funeral the nearest relatives of the deceased attended church, where they remained seated throughout the service. This custom was known as 'taking mourning' and was also observed in Guernsey.

At St. John's Church, Jersey, the church bell is rung at 8 a.m. on the day of a funeral. Originally this was to call the relatives to choose the site of the grave, but now the custom is carried on just to remind parishioners that there is to be a funeral during the day.

The ceremony of homage is rarely performed. In Jersey it is known to have been performed three times—to King Charles II in 1650, King George V in 1921 and Queen Elizabeth II in 1957. In Guernsey the ceremony was performed in 1921 and 1957 and in Sark also in 1957. There is a record of Sir Amias Andros (1610–1674), Lord of the Manor of Sausmarez, Guernsey, and Marshal of the Ceremonies at the Court of King Charles I, paying homage to that Sovereign at Whitehall Palace in 1637.

When the Queen visited Jersey in 1957 the ceremony of homage was held in the Royal Court Room as it had been in 1921. The jurats, greffier, advocates and solicitors, the lords and ladies of the manor who were to make homage, as well as a number of spectators, were all assembled when the Queen entered the court room from the judges' room escorted by the bailiff and the lieutenant-governor and followed by the royal suite. The bailiff explained that certain lords and ladies who held manors and attended twice a year at the Chief Pleas of the Court of Heritage desired to pay homage and asked for permission for them to do so. The Queen, having assented, the roll was called by the Attorney General and the lords and ladies of the manor answered to their names, bowing or curtsying as they did so. When all their names had been called they clasped their hands and together with bowed heads recited the words of homage: "I am your liege man to bear you faith and homage against all." The Lord of St. Ouen, being the senior of those paying homage, stood in front of the Queen and had his hands clasped by hers. At the conclusion of this part of

The Lighthouse on the Casquets off Guernsey

14

the ceremony the Lord of the Manor of Trinity came forward bearing two mallards on a silver dish, which he offered to the Queen and when she had signified her acceptance, he handed the dish to the Receiver-General. This concluded a most interesting occasion. All the formal words in the ceremony were spoken in French.

In passing, it should be mentioned that on her arrival at St. Helier's Harbour the Queen was met by the Lord of Rozel Manor and the Lord of Augrès Manor, in accordance with ancient custom. The Lord of Rozel Manor is one of the Sovereign's hereditary butlers in the island, but he was not called upon on this occasion to carry out the duties of that office as had been the case in 1921; the Lord of Augrès is also an hereditary butler.

In Guernsey the ceremony of homage was held in 1957 at St. George's Hall (now a timber store) and was far more impressive than the Jersey ceremony. The bailiff's procession, which entered the hall preceded by the usher of the Royal Court, consisted of the constables carrying their bâtons (see Chapter IX), the advocates, the greffier, the procureur, the comptroller, the jurats (all walking two by two), the sergeant and lastly the bailiff in his ceremonial robes. After a fanfare of trumpets, the Queen's procession, which consisted of Her Majesty and Prince Philip and the Royal Suite, entered the hall preceded by the Sheriff with drawn sword. As Her Majesty entered the sheriff cried out "Her Majesty and His Royal Highness". After the greffier had said the Lord's Prayer, he read the roll and each member of the Court of Chief Pleas answered to his or her name, rising and bowing as they did so. The bailiff then read the loyal address and presented it on bended knee to the Queen, who then rose and replied. The Lord of the Manor of Sausmarez was then called by the greffier and he mounted the platform, escorted by the lieutenant-governor and the bailiff, and approached the Queen. He then bowed and knelt in front of her and all the lords and ladies who owed homage stood up in their places. With his hands held between those of the Queen the Lord of Sausmarez then spoke the words of homage to which she gave reply. The greffier then called the Lord of the Manor of Les Eperons (the Spurs), and he ascended the platform carrying a crimson and gold cushion on which were the pair of silver-gilt spurs owed by him as his feudal due. The lord of the manor then addressed the Queen stating that he wished to discharge his service and to offer the spurs which he owed for his manor. Then on bended knee he offered the spurs to the Queen, who touched them as a token of acceptance. The Lord of the Manor then rose and withdrew. The proceedings closed by the greffier reading the grace.

The Lord of the Manor of Sausmarez is hereditary Third Butler to the Sovereign, a service performed by the holder of the manor in 1921, but not by the present holder in 1957.

THE FUTURE

As always, perhaps blessedly, the future is a matter for conjecture and no one knows what lies in store for the Channel Islands. The more thinking among the islanders and the residents are concerned about the years ahead. They are very conscious that although the insular economies are booming the present happy state of affairs could change rapidly at any time.

In 1973 the *Report of the Royal Commission on the Constitution, 1969–1973*, sometimes referred to as the 'Kilbrandon Report', was published. Part XI of Volume I of the *Report* deals with the 'Relationships between the United Kingdom and the Channel Islands and the Isle of Man' and at the end of it are set out fourteen main conclusions and recommendations which make no concessions to the basic desire of the insular legislatures to retain the *status quo*. It is not yet known whether all or any of the recommendations contained in the *Report* will be implemented either wholly or in part. It is most unfortunate that at some suitable time after 1945 the insular legislatures did not negotiate with the United Kingdom Government Acts of Parliament reproducing what they considered to be the existing constitutional position and drafted in such a way that generally the implementation of international agreements entered into by the United Kingdom and purporting to extend to the Channel Islands could be effected in the islands only with the consent of the insular legislatures. The States of Jersey in their written evidence proposed an Act of Parliament along those lines, but their proposal did not win the approval of the Commission. Should any British Government endeavour to implement the recommendations of the 'Kilbrandon Report' or anything else which might adversely affect the constitutional position of the islands it will be met with strenuous opposition.

At present Britain's entry into the Common Market has had little effect on the Channel Islands. The terms negotiated by the British Government for the islands were the best which might reasonably have been expected. Most important of all the islands' fiscal arrangements have remained undisturbed. However, these are early days, and in 1974 the British Government sought to re-negotiate Britain's terms of entry. What effect, if any, such re-negotiation or Britain's withdrawal from the Market would have on the islands and their economies is a matter for conjecture.

The Channel Islands have in recent years become recognised as international financial centres and they continue to be, as they have been for many years, tax havens providing some measure of security for the victims of the vicious taxation which obtains in the United Kingdom. The insular authorities are acting in a responsible manner with regard to both these aspects of the economy which are to some extent interrelated, but there is no doubt that there are those in the United Kingdom and elsewhere who would like to put an end to all tax havens, including the Channel Islands.

Apart from constitutional issues and the Common Market, the financial position of the Channel Islands could give cause for concern. Jersey, in particular, although undoubtedly prosperous, has built up a costly administration since it was liberated in 1945, and many considerable (for the size of the island) projects have been carried through which have been largely financed out of revenue. The buildings and administration which have resulted from these projects have to be maintained, and this at ever increasing annual cost. A similar position exists in Guernsey.

The provision of state housing in both Jersey and Guernsey is providing a serious problem for not only is land scarce and consequently expensive, but there is not the money available to finance an endless number of housing projects. The housing shortage is aggravated to some extent by immigration, although housing controls largely contain this aspect of the problem.

On the economic front the insular administrations will have to regulate the local economies with the greatest care for it would be very easy for the prevailing prosperous conditions to change almost overnight. In Jersey, the States are endeavouring by various means to reduce the overheating of the economy, but they must take great care not to convert a thriving situation into a stagnant one. The valuable income derived from taxing wealthy 'residents' might well evaporate if such persons are deterred or prevented from settling in the islands. The lucrative tourist industries which have been painstakingly built up over many years could suffer damage from rising fares, increasing competition, changing tastes and a variety of other factors. The growing and exporting of potatoes, tomatoes, flowers and other crops call for ever greater efficiency on the part of growers and merchants. Any slackening of effort on the part of all engaged in agriculture and horticulture could well result in the decline of these industries.

Fortunately, many, both in the insular governments and in the agricultural and commercial world, are alive to the difficulties that lie ahead, and among them are to be found able men capable of making the right decisions. If the precedents of history are to be followed, a solution will be found to each problem as it arises, and the future can be faced with quiet confidence, but certainly not with complacency.

Whatever happens, nothing can deprive the Channel Islands of either their colourful and eventful history or their natural beauty —whether of countryside or of coastline and sea. They constitute a rich inheritance which neither political nor economic changes can destroy and in this the islands should take comfort.

"O! ever happy Isles!" wrote Michael Drayton, a man born in the reign of the first Elizabeth—may his words ever reflect the true state of the Channel Islands.

SELECT BIBLIOGRAPHY

Alderney Society & Museum, *Bulletin* (Alderney, 1966–   )

Balleine, G. R., *A Biographical Dictionary of Jersey*, Staples Press (London, 1948)

Bois, F. de L., *A Constitutional History*, States of Jersey, (Jersey, 1970)

de Garis, M., *English—Guernsey Dictionary*, La Société Guernesiaise (Guernsey, 1967)

de Gruchy, G. F. B., *Medieval Land Tenures in Jersey*, published privately (Jersey, 1957)

Dobson, R., *Birds of the Channel Islands*, Staples Press (London, 1952)

Eagleston, A. J., *The Channel Islands under Tudor Government*, published for the Guernsey Society at the University Press (Cambridge, 1949)

Ewen, A. H., and de Carteret, A. R., *The Fief of Sark*, The Guernsey Press Co. Ltd., (Guernsey, 1969)

Guernsey Society, *The Quarterly Review* (London, 1944–   )

Guernsey Society, *The Guernsey Farmhouse*, printed for the Society by Thomas De La Rue & Co. Ltd. (London, 1963)

Kendrick, T. D., & Hawkes, A., *The Archaeology of the Channel Islands*, Methuen & Co. Ltd., London, Vol. I. The Bailiwick of Guernsey (Kendrick), 1928, and Vol. II. The Bailiwick of Jersey (Hawkes), 1939

L'Amy, J. H., *Jersey Folk Lore*, Société Jersiaise (Jersey, 1971)

Le Maistre, F., *Dictionnaire Jersiais—Français*, Don Balleine Trust (Jersey, 1966)

Lemprière, R., *History of the Channel Islands*, Robert Hale (London, 1974)

Le Patourel, J. H., *Medieval Administration of the Channel Islands 1199–1399*, Oxford University Press (London, 1937)

MacCulloch, E., *Guernsey Folk Lore* (edited by E. F. Carey), Elliot Stock (London, 1903)

Mayne, R. H., *Old Channel Islands Silver—Its Makers and Marks* (Print Holdings and Investments Ltd.) (Jersey, 1969)

Sinel, L. P., *The German Occupation of Jersey*, Corgi Books (Transworld Publishers Ltd.) (London, 1969)

Société Guernesiaise (formerly The Guernsey Society of Natural Science and Local Research), *Report and Transactions* (1882–   )

Société Jersiaise, *Bulletin Annuel* (Jersey, 1875–   )

Stevens, J., *Old Jersey Houses*, privately printed (Jersey, 1966)

Wood, A. & M., *Islands in Danger*, Four Square Books (The New English Library Ltd.) (London, 1967)

INDEX

The following abbreviations are used in the Index: A = Alderney; G = Guernsey; H = Herm; J = Jersey; S = Sark.